The Amazon Rain Forest

Look for these and other books in the
Lucent Endangered Animals and Habitats series:

The Amazon Rain Forest
The Bald Eagle
The Elephant
The Giant Panda
The Oceans
The Rhinoceros
Seals and Sea Lions
The Shark
The Tiger
The Whale
The Wolf

Other related titles in the Lucent Overview series:

Acid Rain
Endangered Species
Energy Alternatives
Garbage
The Greenhouse Effect
Hazardous Waste
Ocean Pollution
Oil Spills
Ozone
Pesticides
Population
Rainforests
Recycling
Vanishing Wetlands
Zoos

THE AMAZON RAIN FOREST

BY DARV JOHNSON

Endangered Animals & Habitats

LUCENT BOOKS, INC.
SAN DIEGO, CALIFORNIA

Library of Congress Cataloging-in-Publication Data

Johnson, Darv, 1971–
      The Amazon rain forest / by Darv Johnson.
          p.   cm. — (Lucent overview series) (Endangered animals and
      habitats)
      Includes bibliographical references (p.   ) and index.
      Summary: Discusses the destruction of the Amazon rain forest
and details the efforts to save it.
      ISBN 1-56006-369-6   (lib. bdg. : alk. paper)
      1. Rain forest ecology—Amazon River Region—Juvenile
literature.   2. Endangered ecosystems—Amazon River Region—
Juvenile literature.   3. Rain forest conservation—Amazon River
Region—Juvenile literature.   4. Deforestation—Amazon River
Region—Juvenile literature.   [1. Rain forest ecology—Amazon
River Region. 2. Ecology—Amazon River Region. 3. Conservation
of natural resources.]   I. Title.   II. Series.   III. Series:
Endangered animals & habitats.
QH112.J64   1999
577.34'0981'1—dc21   98-35272
                                                                 CIP
                                                                  AC

FEB 0 2 2000
Copyright © 1999 by Lucent Books, Inc.
P.O. Box 289011, San Diego, CA 92198-9011
Printed in the U.S.A.

Contents

Introduction

FOR MANY PEOPLE the phrase "Amazon rain forest" triggers an image of a single, gigantic forest. A view of the Amazon from the air, spreading out in all directions like a vast green carpet, supports that idea. But a closer inspection reveals that the green carpet that seems endless and impenetrable from above is not one giant forest but a collection of many smaller ones. The Amazon varies constantly as it moves up mountains and away from rivers. Each acre contains new and different types of trees, shrubs, ferns, and soils.

As the forest varies, so do the insects and animals that live within it. Each species has unique qualities and characteristics that have allowed it to survive. For example, monkeys have teeth specially designed to open shells. Moths and butterflies have long tongues that reach into flowers in search of pollen, and jaguars have spotted coats that allow them to hide easily in the forest.

Evolution and disruption

The process by which these special characteristics develop over millions of years is called evolution. A tree with bitterly poisonous leaves today probably had no protection from animals that wanted to eat it long ago. Over time the tree developed the poison to defend itself. Some of the animal species that dined on it gradually developed the ability to digest the new poisons, while others died off. After centuries of this tug-of-war, the result is a standoff: a tree with bitter, poisonous leaves and only one or two animal species that are capable of digesting them.

While some changes in the rain forest take thousands of years, others happen in just seconds. Even the strongest tree will eventually fall to disease, old age, or a tropical storm. As it crashes to the ground, the vines in its branches strain and tighten on other trees and pull them down as well. In an instant, the home of thousands of birds, snakes, insects, monkeys, and frogs is destroyed.

Usually the rain forest can adjust to the change. Insects and animals find new homes after a tree falls, and plants spring to life in the newfound sunlight. Small trees burst up into the gap, spreading out leaves and branches. Eventually, the forest is whole again.

Change is a natural part of the Amazon rain forest. Over the last three decades, however, the pace of change has quickened. Millions of people have invaded the Amazon in search of timber, minerals, oil, and other riches. As humans move deeper into the forest, they disrupt the natural

Although the dense emerald canopy of the Amazon rain forest looks like one huge mass when viewed from above, it actually contains a variety of habitats.

Logging poses a major problem to the survival of the rain forest. The demand for exotic hardwoods such as mahogany have hastened the destruction of forest life.

balance of loss and recovery. Their chain saws and bulldozers fell trees more easily than do storms and disease. They rip out chunks of the forest faster than animals and insects can adapt and faster than trees can grow back.

The loss of the Amazon is felt far beyond the borders of the forest itself. It has an impact on science, medicine, and perhaps even the temperature of the entire planet. For this reason, many people think of the Amazon as part of a "global commons." They put it in the same category as the world's oceans, or the North and South Poles—areas so large and important that their continued existence is critical to everyone, from a forest tribesman in Brazil to a suburban teenager half a world away.

1

Nature's Hothouse

LOOPING OVER SOUTHEAST ASIA, central and West Africa, Australia, and Latin America, tropical rain forests form a green belt around the equator. Taken together, they cover only about 8 percent of the earth's surface. But tropical rain forests are by far the earth's richest environment. Packed into this relatively small area is the most amazing collection of plant, animal, and insect species found in nature. More than one-half of all plant and animal species on the earth make their homes in tropical rain forests.

The Amazon rain forest is the largest of all tropical rain forests. Bigger than all the others combined, the Amazon sprawls across 2.3 million square miles—an area nearly as large as the United States. It carpets giant portions of Brazil, Bolivia, Peru, Ecuador, Venezuela, and Colombia and spills over the borders of French Guinea, Guiana, and Suriname. From the foothills of the Andes Mountains on the western edge of South America, it stretches more than 2,000 miles east to the Atlantic Ocean.

Those who study the plant and animal species of the Amazon rain forest are faced with overwhelming numbers. Eighty thousand plant species are found in the Amazon, as compared to the 1,200 that can be found in all of New England. Some 297 different kinds of tree have been identified on just 2½ acres in Brazil, while the same amount of forest in California might contain only 10 tree species. An estimated 900 bird species make their home in the Amazon, ranging from tiny hummingbirds to giant eagles. As new areas of the rain forest are explored and researched, new species are being discovered almost faster than scientists can classify them. The biologist Edward O. Wilson, who once found 43 different ant species on a single tree stump, writes, "Every time I enter a previously unstudied stretch of rain forest, I find a new species . . . within a day or two, sometimes during the first hour."[1]

For over two centuries, this tremendous diversity has been a source of wonder for scientists and naturalists, and many theories have been offered to explain it. Some scientists point to the great age of the Amazon rain forest. Because it has existed relatively unchanged for tens of millions of years, they argue, its inhabitants have developed into highly specialized creatures, each performing jobs that are critical to the health of the forest. Other scientists believe that a series of floods swept over the Amazon basin long ago, creating islands where drastically different species developed. As the flood waters receded, these is-

A Truly Exciting Find

A small marmoset is one of six new monkey species discovered in the Amazon since 1990. Only six inches in length and weighing six ounces, scientists believe it is the world's second smallest monkey. "Finding a new beetle in the rainforest may not be surprising, but finding a new monkey is truly exciting," Russell Mittermeier of Conservation International stated in a June 18, 1996, *New York Times* article. As humans push farther into unexplored areas of the rain forest, Mittermeier is certain that more discoveries are on the way. "I wouldn't be surprised if we found another five monkeys by the year 2000," he said.

Six inches long and weighing six ounces, the pygmy marmoset is believed to be the world's second smallest species of monkey.

lands and all of their species were rejoined to form the Amazon of today.

Regardless of the origins of this diversity, the Amazon provides ideal habitat for all types of life. Nineteenth-century biologist Charles Darwin, after his first visit to the Amazon, described it as "one great, wild, untidy, luxuriant hothouse, made by Nature for herself."[2] The key to growth in the Amazon is its unvarying heat and humidity. The temperature remains at about eighty degrees, despite the season, making it cooler than a New York or Florida summer. The presence of rain is also a constant. Even in the dry season, the Amazon usually receives at least four inches of rain per month. During the rainy season, almost every afternoon brings a heavy downpour lasting several hours. Some areas of the Amazon, like the Chocó of Colombia, receive more than twenty-four feet of rain every year.

The combination of constant heat and humidity creates ideal growing conditions. Free from freezing temperatures and long periods without rain, plants grow rapidly all year, as if they were contained in a greenhouse.

The Amazon River is the lifeblood of the rain forest. Ten times bigger than the Mississippi River, the Amazon is two

A typical afternoon downpour during the rainy season can last several hours. At least four inches of rain usually fall every thirty days even during the dry months.

hundred miles wide at its mouth and moves enough fresh water every second to supply ten New York Citys for a year. Like the forest that it supports, the Amazon River is home to an astounding variety of life. Of the five thousand freshwater fish species on earth, two thousand can be found in the Amazon River.

When the river floods, it drastically alters the landscape of the rain forest. Rising by as much as fifty feet in places, the river turns low-lying areas into flooded forests, or *varzeas*. For up to ten months every year, floodwaters cover the smaller trees in these areas, and only the tops of the tallest trees are visible.

Many fish have adapted to the unusual habitat of the *varzea*. Some fish feed on plant seeds and spread them over a wide range, just as birds, insects, and bats do in an unflooded forest. One such fish, the tambaqui, uses its powerful jaws and huge molars to crush and eat the rock-hard seeds of the rubber tree. Other fish enjoy the easy access to insects. The arowana, for example, leaps high out of the water to pluck beetles off of tree branches.

The pink river dolphin, or boto, is also well suited to life in the flooded forest. Ranging in color from rosy to a brilliant pink, the chubby marine mammal differs from other dolphins because its neck vertebrae are not fused together. This adaptation makes it easier for the boto to twist its way through the narrow passages formed by submerged trees. Its ability to paddle forward with one flipper while back-paddling with the other also adds to its maneuverability.

The high, muddy water carries a heavy load of dirt and soil from the foothills of the Andes Mountains. Rich in nutrients, the soil left behind by the high water allows lush vegetation to grow.

The roof of the rain forest

Three-quarters of all Amazonian creatures live more than one hundred feet above the ground in the rain forest canopy. Intense competition for light makes the trees that form the canopy extremely tall and straight. The branches are concentrated at the top, where they spread out to gather light. Packed together, these branches form a roof that prevents moisture from escaping and sunlight from entering the rain forest.

Emergent trees, the biggest trees in the forest, thrust through the canopy and into open air. Although they are exposed to the high winds and lightning of tropical storms, they are rewarded by an abundant supply of sunlight. Raptors like the harpy eagle, which has claws the size of a human hand, nest in the emergent trees and scan for prey from the high branches.

Floodwaters carry nutrient-rich soil from the Andes Mountains to the lowland areas of the rain forest, providing nourishment for trees and other plant life.

Epiphytes, fruits, and flowers

The plants and animals of the canopy provide many examples of the interdependence of species that makes the Amazon so unique. Epiphytes, or "air plants" as they are sometimes called, are plants that cling to the trees in the canopy without relying on them for nutrients. Instead, these plants draw food and moisture from the bark of trees or directly from the air. A single rain forest tree may hold thousands of epiphytes, including orchids, plants that use their spectacular flowers to attract bees and butterflies.

The leaves of bromeliads, another type of epiphyte, form a cup capable of holding gallons of water. Far above the forest floor, bromeliad pools provide a feeding and breeding ground for hundreds of creatures. Insects and frogs lay eggs and raise their young in bromeliad pools, while snakes, lizards, birds, and monkeys visit pools in search of food and water to drink.

Bromeliads and other epiphytes also help the trees that host them. As plants and animals that live in epiphytes die and rot, they become a rich source of nutrients. Trees send roots down from their branches to these epiphyte gardens and draw the nutrients away.

This emergent tree has pierced the forest canopy in search of sunlight. Its high branches serve as perches for harpy eagles and other birds of prey.

"We think that epiphytes are probably a keystone species,"[3] says Nalina Nadkarni, a biologist who climbs into one-hundred-foot trees to study the rain forest canopy. A keystone species performs a function so important to an ecosystem that, if that species were to disappear, other species would die out or move away.

The process of pollination, by which many plants reproduce themselves, faces special challenges in the canopy of the Amazon. Many plants are separated from others of the same species by hundreds of feet, and there is little wind to spread pollen from plant to plant. "Pollination is not a chance event in the rainforest," writes Ghillean Prance, director of the Royal Botanical Gardens. "It is a precise delivery of a tiny dust-like grain to another flower of the same species over a distance of hundreds of feet. This is only possible because of the way in which plants and animals have evolved together in a mutually dependent life style."[4]

Bees, bats, hummingbirds, and beetles serve as pollinators for the beautiful and strong-smelling flowers in the canopy. The partnerships formed between plants and animals provide equal benefits to both. For example, a night-flying bat with poor vision but a keen sense of smell is attracted to a pale, strong-smelling flower. As the bat feeds on the flower's nectar, its snout is covered in pollen. Over the course of the night, the bat transfers this pollen to other plants of the same species. The plants, in turn, use this pollen to create seeds that will grow into more plants. In this way the bat feeds itself while helping the plant to reproduce. Neither species could survive without the other.

Other plants use hard-shelled seeds to reproduce and depend on certain types of monkeys, birds, and bats to act as seed dispersers. After eating a fruit in one tree, the dispersers deposit the indigestible seeds in their droppings in

 ### Rafting the Rain Forest

Since climbing ropes are too dangerous, and towers and walkways do not get him close enough to his subject, French scientist Francis Hallé decided to study the rain forest canopy from the comfort of a giant rubber raft. Hallé's raft is constructed from inflatable rubber pontoons with netting strung in between them, and it is light enough to rest on top of the canopy trees. Climbing through the netting, Hallé and his scientists collect specimens and study plant and insect life. Occasionally they even sleep in the raft. When they want to study a different part of the canopy, a dirigible tows the raft to the new site.

A long-tongued bat enjoys an on-the-fly feast of nectar. As the bat feeds, it transfers pollen to other blooms, helping the plants to reproduce.

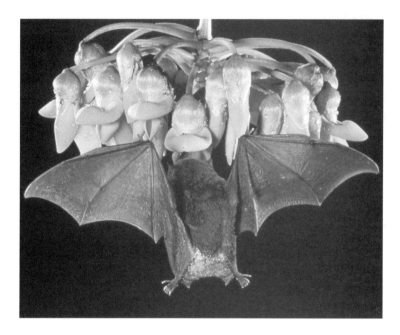

another part of the forest. The seeds are now far from where they started, increasing the plant's chances for survival.

Toucans and macaws are the most beautiful of the seed dispersers. With its enormous and colorful bill, the toucan resembles a cartoon bird as it flies through the canopy. Because its bill is made out of the same material as human fingernails, it is actually quite light in weight, and its sharp edges make it the perfect tool for feasting on ripe fruits. The macaw, a colorful species of parrot, is also armed with a strong beak to crack open even the hardest nutshells. Animals like these ensure that Amazonian plants can distribute themselves over a wide area to guard against insects and plagues.

For those creatures not interested in fruits and flowers, the canopy offers plenty of leaves to eat. But because leaves are difficult to digest, few creatures can make a meal of them. One that can is the two-toed sloth. With claws like hooks and limbs shaped like hangers, the sloth is perfectly adapted to a life spent hanging upside down from trees and feeding on leaves. The slow motions of the sloth, combined with a greenish algae that grows in its fur, make it difficult for predators to spot.

The howler monkey uses a special compartment in its stomach to digest tree leaves. Like the sloth, it rarely needs to visit the forest floor. The howler speeds from tree to tree, using its tail as a fifth limb to grasp onto branches. Its name comes from the eerie noise it makes to mark its territory.

The struggle for light

The understory is a layer of immature trees and shrubs growing in the deep shade of the canopy. In the dark, cool, and humid air, these trees grow large leaves to take advantage of the small amount of light that trickles through and wait for a hole to appear in the canopy.

The tremendous crash of a canopy tree tumbling to the earth signals the beginning of a furious fight for light among the trees and plants in the understory. When a taller tree falls, an understory tree puts out leaves and branches to soak up sun and, with this sudden jolt of energy, leaps upward to fill the gap. Its branches spread out to prevent sunlight from reaching competing trees, which then fall back and die. After several decades, the tree reaches the canopy, and the forest is healed and stable again.

Large, woody vines called lianas use a different strategy to gain access to sunlight. Lianas sprout up out of the soil and grow through the understory to the canopy above. In their rush for light, lianas do not stop long enough to grow trunks. Instead, they climb the trunks of tall trees winding around and around to reach the canopy. Or they may latch on to a young tree, and hang on as the tree grows towards the light.

Lianas can grow to be thousands of feet long and form tangled webs between neighboring trees in the canopy. When one tree falls, the lianas it carries may pull other trees down as well. Some trees have adapted to this threat by shedding bark and branches that are filled with lianas and other vines.

A keel-billed toucan displays its immense beak. Used for crushing ripe fruit, the bill is made of the same material as human fingernails and is remarkably lightweight.

Partnerships in the Amazon do not always provide benefits to each species involved. Known in Spanish as the *matapolo*, or "tree-killer," the strangler fig preys on the very trees it depends on to survive. Beginning life in the canopy, the strangler fig sends its roots down to the ground, wrapping itself tightly around a tree trunk. The strangler fig soon covers the entire trunk of the tree, blocking the light and water the tree needs to survive. Dozens of years later, when the host tree dies and rots away, the strangler fig remains standing, hollow but healthy. By taking over its host's position in the canopy, it has claimed a temporary victory in the never-ending struggle for light.

The forest that feeds itself

A constant shower of dead leaves, twigs, and branches falls from the lush vegetation of the canopy to the forest floor. In the central Amazon, twenty-two pounds of plant matter may fall on a single square yard of earth every year. But the soil of the rain forest is not thick and dark with rotted leaves; instead, it is extremely thin and so lacking in nutrients that in some places it resembles white sand. The complex process that makes the fallen leaves vanish is another example of interdependence in the rain forest.

In the warm, wet air of the Amazon, dead leaves and animals rot away quickly. A leaf on the forest floor disappears fifty to sixty times faster than it

The strangler fig is a parasitic plant that eventually covers every inch of the tree trunk on which it lives, starving the tree of the light and nutrients it needs to survive.

does in a North American forest. Millions of scavenging insects living on the forest floor speed the process. Leafcutter ants attack a fallen leaf, chopping it into small chunks. They use their strong jaws to carry the pieces back to their underground nest. Once there, ants chew the leaf pieces and feed them to fungi. To feed themselves, the ants then eat the fungi.

Earthworms, flies, bees, wasps, maggots, beetles, and even cockroaches join the ants as decomposers. Decomposers feed on dead plants and animals. As they digest the decaying matter, nutrients such as potassium and phosphorus are released. Green plants then use these nutrients to fuel their growth. "Without decomposers, life would eventually grind to a halt for lack of nutrients,"[5] writes Mark Collins. Given their important function, it is not surprising that insects are found in such huge numbers in the Amazon. In fact, in terms of sheer weight, insects represent the largest amount of living material in the rain forest, except for the trees and plants themselves.

Insects do not work alone to break down plant material. Mycorrhiza is a threadlike combination of plant roots and fungi. It covers tree roots, dead leaves, insects, and animals found atop the soil. Mycorrhiza's function is to break down and digest dead materials and return the nutrients they contain to the trees.

Insects and fungi play an important role in helping the forest feed itself. Plants need minerals such as phosphorus and potassium to grow. In the forests of the United States, plants draw these nutrients from the thick, rich soils. But in the Amazon rain forest, almost all of the nutrients are found in the living plants and animals. The rain forest's ability to recycle these nutrients quickly and efficiently is what allows it to survive.

 Insect Expert Terry Erwin

Terry Erwin is an entomologist—a scientist who studies insects. On a small plot of rain forest in Ecuador, Erwin spreads out a sheet of nylon and sprays a cloud of insecticide into the rain forest canopy. All the insects that fall from the trees are taken back to Washington, where they are sorted and studied. Out of any given sample, four out of five species have never before been seen by entomologists. Based on his research, Erwin estimates that just two and a half acres of rain forest contain fifty to sixty thousand species of insects and spiders.

The Secret Life of Anacondas

How do you calm an angry snake? It helps to have an extra sock handy. In the rain forests of Venezuela, a team of researchers is studying the feeding and mating habits of the anaconda. After capturing one of the giant snakes, the scientists place a sock over its head. The sock has a soothing effect and makes it easier for the scientists to transport the snake to their laboratory.

The longest snake they have found stretched to 17½ feet, while the heaviest tipped the scales at 214 pounds. Anacondas reach this size on a steady diet of ducks, large rodents called capybaras, and deer. The victims are normally swallowed head-first. Occasionally, however, the snakes choose inappropriate snacks. In an April 2, 1996, *New York Times* article, one scientist reported finding a dead deer with teeth marks from the anaconda on its head. Apparently, the snake had tried repeatedly to swallow the deer, only to be defeated in its efforts by the heavy set of antlers on the deer's head.

Four natives struggle under the weight of an anaconda they have just helped capture for scientists to study.

While the forest floor is a haven for insect and fungi species, it is less welcoming to large mammals. The lack of available food makes it difficult for them to survive. The big animals that do live on the ground are found in small numbers and are hard to see. Where a ray of light breaks through a hole in the canopy, deer feed on the new growth of shrubs and grasses. Big cats such as ocelots and jaguars use their dappled coats to blend into the shadows, hoping to make the deer their next meal.

Attracted to the sound of fruit falling from a Brazil nut tree, large rodents called agoutis eat many of the seeds from the fruit and then bury the leftovers. Because agoutis often forget where they bury food, some of the seeds are able to grow into new Brazil nut trees. Other creatures, including a type of wild pig called a peccary and the paca, a twenty-two-pound rodent that growls like a dog, join the agouti in the hunt for fallen fruits.

Snakes are closely associated with the Amazon rain forest in many people's minds, and a wide variety of types are present there. Anacondas are giant snakes that can grow to be over thirty feet long. Like boa constrictors, they eat birds, peccaries, crocodiles, or any other animal that they can wrap themselves around. They kill their prey by squeezing them to death with their powerful bodies.

The fer-de-lance, another species of snake, is perhaps the most deadly creature of the Amazon. Prowling the forest floor, the fer-de-lance does not use its eyes to find its prey. Instead, it uses a heat-sensing organ located in its head. Once it has discovered a small mammal or other creature, the fer-de-lance kills it with a venom that can also be lethal to humans.

Humans in the Amazon

With millions of species spread over millions of square miles, the Amazon rain forest may appear to be indestructible. But as Edward Wilson notes, it is really a delicately balanced "house of cards."[6] Each plant and animal species plays a small but important role in the smooth operation of the forest as a whole. Take away one type of bird, for example, and the trees that rely on it as a pollinator will die. As the trees fall to the ground, all of the species that feed on or live in them will suffer as well.

A fer-de-lance snake delivers a killing blow to a whiptail lizard. The snake's deadly venom can also be fatal to humans.

Armed with chain saws and bulldozers, humans are moving rapidly into this complex system. The Amazon is being cut down faster than it can heal itself, and the species it supports are being destroyed. As plants and animals disappear, the house of cards is becoming less stable. Each acre that is cleared brings it closer to collapse.

2

The Amazon in Peril

FOR ALL OF the Amazon rain forest's beauty, it is the promise of wealth that has drawn people most strongly into its depths. Since the first Europeans visited the Amazon in the sixteenth century, explorers and adventurers have marched into the forest in search of hidden diamonds and silver or mythical cities made of gold. The legend of El Dorado, an Amazonian king said to be so wealthy that his body was adorned with gold dust, was alone powerful enough to launch dozens of expeditions.

For others, the Amazon held more practical promises. Many were convinced that the vast wilderness, home to such a rich variety of plant and animal life, would be ideal for farming and ranching. The English naturalist Alfred Russel Wallace wrote of the Amazon after his visit in the 1850s: "I fearlessly assert that here the 'primeval' forest can be converted into rich pasture and meadow land, into cultivated fields, gardens and orchards, containing every variety of produce with half the labour."[7]

While minerals are what drew many to the Amazon, its first economic boom came from an unexpected source—rubber. For many years, the raw material for manufacturing rubber could be found only in the wild rubber trees of the Amazon. As a result, the region held a monopoly on the world supply. From the late 1800s until the 1930s, rubber flowed out of the rain forest and into Europe and the United States, where it was fashioned into car and bicycle tires and countless other products. In exchange, millions of dollars flowed into the major cities of the Amazon. Grand

Americans, Rubber, and the Amazon

The story of rubber in the Amazon begins with an American named Nelson Goodyear. In 1842 Goodyear invented vulcanization, the process that made rubber such a useful and valuable product. Brazil had the only supply of rubber trees in the world at the time and so profited enormously. They guarded the seeds of their wild rubber trees carefully so that other nations would not be able to grow them and compete in the rubber trade. With the help of a corrupt customs official, a British botanist smuggled seeds from the Amazon out of the country in the late 1800s. Large plantations were created in Malaysia and Indonesia, and the Amazon rubber monopoly was broken.

Another famous American was deeply involved in Amazonian rubber. In 1927 the American automaker Henry Ford set up Fordlandia—a seven thousand-acre rubber plantation in the heart of the Amazon. The trees were quickly destroyed by insects and disease. Eighteen years later Ford sold his $10 million investment to the Brazilian government for just $500,000.

Nelson Goodyear, the inventor of the vulcanization process which turned raw rubber into a valuable commodity.

opera houses and mansions were built with the fortunes that were made.

The strong economy did not last. By World War I the British and Dutch had learned how to grow rubber on giant plantations in Southeast Asia. The price of rubber plummeted, and the Amazon was abandoned again.

Many other industries tried and failed to maintain a foothold in the Amazon. Thousands of explorers and speculators returned from the forest empty-handed. As a result, the Amazon was relatively intact well into the twentieth century, even after more than four hundred years of attempts at settlement. Only in the 1960s did the development and destruction of the Amazon begin in earnest, and at an alarming rate. This dramatic invasion by people was largely the result of decisions made by the Brazilian government.

Occupying the Amazon

Brazilian political leaders have long viewed the Amazon as a treasure chest of timber, minerals, and other riches. At the same time, the Brazilian portion of the forest was seen as a liability to the security of the nation—a vast empty territory that neighboring armies could easily enter and occupy. In the 1960s, with a failing economy and a poverty-stricken population, the military-led government decided it would take drastic steps both to capitalize on this resource and secure its borders. The result was a sweeping campaign to settle the Amazon. In the words of Brazilian general Castillo Branco in 1964, "Amazonian occupation will proceed as though we are waging a strategically conducted war."[8]

The destruction of the rain forest began with the construction of highways. The Amazon's size, and the difficulties it posed to transportation, had long been its best defense. Without roads, it was too difficult and expensive to transport goods to and from the rain forest. To solve this problem three major highway projects were built by the Brazilian government, penetrating into eastern, central, and western Amazonia. The largest of these was the Trans-Amazon. Built during the 1970s, it cut a path 230 feet wide and 2,000 miles long through the heart of the rain forest.

Behind the slogan Land Without People for People Without Land, the Brazilian government lured poor families from its overcrowded cities into the Amazon. Settlers followed the new highways, drawn by the government's promise of free land to farm. They were offered transportation, food supplies, and money to help them while they established their farms. They were also promised schools, housing, medical supplies, and technical assistance.

The relocation effort has been very successful in bringing people to the Amazon. More than half of the 16 million people currently living in the Amazon moved there in the thirty years since the campaign began. Relocation has come at great cost, however. The new settlers, practicing a type of farming known as slash-and-burn, have had a disastrous effect on the health of the forest.

Brazil and the Trans-Amazon Highway

Slash-and-burn

Before settlers can farm in the Amazon, the forest must be cleared. Vines, shrubs, and small trees are cut first, followed by the large trees of the canopy. The downed vegetation is burned after it dries out sufficiently.

Burning is the fastest way to clear the debris away. It also releases the nutrients stored in the vegetation into the soil. Crops are planted just after the burning to take advantage of the burst of nitrogen and other fuel.

The burnings are a way of life in Amazonian nations. For four to five months every year, the blazes rage in the forest. If the forest is unusually dry, these fires can burn out of control. Satellites recorded forty-five thousand fires in a five-month period of 1997 alone. When added together, these fires covered an area as large as New Jersey.

Until recently, Brazilian law all but required clearing. It was the only way for settlers to gain the title, or legal ownership, of the land that they were farming. Land that was not cleared was labeled "unproductive" and reclaimed by the government. Uncleared land is also undesirable for another reason. It is far more likely to be occupied by squatters; poor farmers who settle on land and begin to use it regardless of whether it belongs to them.

Poor soil conditions

Poor soils make slash-and-burn farming even more destructive. Because Amazonian soils contain so few nutrients, they cannot support more than one or two harvests. The land becomes dry, choked with weeds, and unsuitable for farming. A family may spend less than two years farming a plot of land before moving on to another untouched piece of forest. There the cycle begins again.

The settlers suffer as much as the rain forest. Farming the tropical soils is difficult, and the rewards are small. The amount of money that settlers receive for a good crop of rice or coffee may not even cover the costs of planting it. Many settlers cannot grow enough to feed themselves. They are soon forced to return to the poverty-stricken cities from which they came. "When we arrived, the only hope I saw for us was the land here," says Angel Ordonez, a farmer in the Ecuadorian Amazon. "We have worked harder than animals. But it hasn't served for anything."[9]

An effective yet environmentally costly method of clearing land for farming, slash-and-burn results in the loss of thousands of square miles of rain forest every year.

Cattle ranching

Land abandoned by farmers often ends up in the hands of cattle ranchers. Nearly three-quarters of the land cleared in the Amazon is eventually turned over to livestock. The large-scale attempts at cattle ranching in the Amazon began in the mid-1960s. It was then that the Brazilian government took note of the rising demand for beef in Brazil and around the world. Hoping to capitalize on this trend, the government chose the Amazon as the best location for an enormous new beef industry.

Ranchers were attracted to the rain forest by tax breaks, favorable loans, and other financial incentives. At one point the government offered ranchers one free acre of forest for every three that they cleared. The World Bank offered loans to jump-start new cattle ranches, and foreign corporations added their money and expertise to the endeavor.

Today there are 8 million head of cattle in the Brazilian Amazon alone, matching the number found on the fertile pastures of Nebraska. While this number is impressive, it does not tell the whole story. Only three out of one hundred cattle ranches in the Amazon ever make a profit. Along the Belém-Brasília highway, 90 percent of all new cattle ranches go out of business within eight years. Amazonian cows cannot be exported because they have hoof-and-mouth disease. In fact, the Amazon region remains a net importer of beef, unable to produce enough to feed even the people who live in the rain forest.

Cattle ranching in the rain forest is made difficult by many of the same factors that discourage farming. Poor soils are unable to withstand the punishment of a herd of cattle. The trampling hooves quickly tear up pasture and grassland, rendering the land useless. Within a few years, the number of acres required to support a single cow jumps from two and a half to ten or more. The constant demand for unspoiled land drives ranchers deeper into the forest.

In reality, most of the large cattle ranchers are not too concerned with making money by raising cows. The land is what they are really interested in. In the high-inflation economy of Brazil, large land holdings in the Amazon are an excellent investment. Keeping cattle on the land is often nothing more than a way to demonstrate ownership of the land and to claim the tax breaks and beneficial loans offered by the government.

Flooding the forest

While farmers and ranchers scratch a living from the rain forest soil, others seek to profit from the Amazon's water resources. With its abundant rivers, the Amazon is an excellent site for hydroelectric dams. The dams produce power by harnessing the force of rivers and using it to turn large turbines.

The Tucuruí dam under construction. Once completed, it submerged nearly fifteen hundred square miles of rain forest.

The construction of each dam has a devastating impact on the environment. The Tucuruí dam in eastern Amazonia flooded nearly fifteen hundred square miles of rain forest. The billion-dollar Balbina dam, on the Uatumã River in Brazil, flooded nine hundred square miles of forest with water just a few feet deep. Despite its huge size, the Balbina produces a tiny amount of energy relative to its environmental and financial costs.

Brazil's plan for hydropower in the Amazon calls for additional dams that would flood a minimum of two thousand additional square miles of rain forest if built. According to one expert, the flooding only marks the beginning of the destruction: "Hydroelectric projects affect much more than what they flood. Roads are built to all dams, which often are in remote places, and those roads bring in people who cut the forest."[10] Dams also block the passage of fish, and destroy the vegetation and habitat that millions of plants and animals need to survive.

An Animal Relocation Program

As trees disappear under water, so does the habitat for thousands of animals. What becomes of these creatures when their homes are flooded? Before the Samuel dam in Brazil was completed, relocation crews were ordered to capture and move as many animals as possible from the area to be flooded.

In editor Martha C. Christian's book *Emerald Realm: Earth's Precious Rain Forests*, ecologist Richard Bierregaard calls these relocation programs ineffective:

> Crews take anything they can find, tear sloths and monkeys out of trees, then just let them go at the base of the dam. The animals run into the forest, where there are already plenty of sloths and monkeys, and in come another hundred. Dumping animals into territories of other animals is *not* a good thing to do.

In spite of the damage, environmentalists do not condemn all dams. Dams produce power in a way that is cleaner than a coal, oil, or nuclear plant. At the same time, a well-placed dam such as the Tucuruí can supply cheap power to a large area. Its presence might prevent the need for more coal mining or oil exploration in another part of the forest.

Hidden wealth

The power produced by hydroelectric dams draws other types of economic development into the Amazon. For example, cheap and abundant power from dams fuels gigantic mining operations deep in the heart of the rain forest. Started in the 1980s, the Grande Carajás mine in the eastern Amazon sprawls across 324,000 square miles—an area bigger than Texas. It is one of the most valuable concentrations of minerals on earth. Miners at the site have uncovered one-third of the world's high quality iron ore as well as large amounts of copper, gold, nickel, and other valuable minerals.

With chain saws, bulldozers, and dynamite, mining companies peel away the forest to uncover the wealth below. The destruction does not stop with the mines themselves. The iron that is extracted must be refined in giant wood-burning smelters. The fires of Grande Carajás's twenty-four planned iron smelters will consume an estimated 10 million tons of wood each year, an amount equal to six hundred square miles of standing rain forest.

The Amazon also attracts a special type of fortune hunter known in Brazil as a *garimpeiro*. *Garimpeiros* use shovels and explosives to probe for gold in streams and rivers. They are usually young men aged fifteen to twenty-five, and they work alone or in small groups.

Many have fled urban slums or poor farms with the slim hope of striking it rich in the rain forest. "Look at it this way," says one *garimpeiro*, "if I buy a ticket in the lottery, I have one chance in a couple of million, right? Here in Serra Pelada [a large gold mine] it's one in a thousand, maybe less. The way I see it, life's a gamble, and I'm just following the odds."[11]

There are more than five hundred thousand of these miners in the Amazon. Each one depends on the rain forest for firewood, food, and lodging. Though their individual impact is small, together they add greatly to the destruction.

They also add a deadly poison, mercury, to the environment. *Garimpeiros* use mercury to separate gold from other soil. Unfortunately, mercury is extremely toxic to humans. Over time it builds up in the blood of those who are exposed to it. The symptoms of mercury poisoning can be horrific and include brain damage and birth defects. No one knows how many miners, settlers, or tribal people have been exposed to mercury poisoning.

Mercury also harms the plants and animals of the rain forest. Increasingly, it is being found in water, fish, and aquatic birds. Wetlands, parks, and wildlife refuges far from the mines where mercury is used have also been contaminated. As new deposits of gold are discovered and the *garimpeiros* flock to mine them, mercury will continue to spread throughout the Amazon.

Oil in the Amazon

Oil is another valuable resource hidden below the surface of the rain forest. In Ecuador the discovery of oil has attracted the interest of major corporations. The revenue from this oil is critical to Ecuador's economy, providing half of the government's revenue. But the oil drilling pollutes rivers and streams. Chemicals are spilled, gas fires fill the air with smoke, and pipelines crisscross the forest.

During the 1970s and 1980s Texaco, a giant American company, ravaged large areas of the Ecuadoran Amazon in its search for new well sites. It left behind a messy trail of toxic chemicals, polluted streams, and damaged forests. By some estimates, the company pumped 5 million gallons of waste into rivers and streams every day for almost twenty-five years.

Texaco is quick to defend its actions in the rain forest. "We complied with existing laws and regulations,"[12] says Michael Trevino, a spokesman for the company. Angry environmentalists accuse Texaco of drilling without regard for the forest or the people who live there and of taking advantage of the weak environmental laws in Ecuador. "Now the $5 billion profit that Texaco took away is being paid by the indigenous people of Ecuador," charges Cristobal Bonifaz, an attorney who filed suit against the company in an attempt to make it pay for the damage it caused. "Texaco walked out and left a disaster."[13] Though clean-ups ordered by the court are underway, the scars of oil exploration in the Amazon will not be easily erased.

Logging

The fastest-growing threat to the Amazon rain forest is logging. In the past the forests of Southeast Asia and Africa supplied much of the world with tropical timber. These forests have already nearly disappeared due to intense logging. The Amazon now represents the largest remaining supply of highly valued tropical timber in the world.

Trees cut in the Amazon often end up as furniture, cardboard, and books in the United States, Europe, and Asia. Developed nations have a huge appetite for wood and paper products. The average person in the United States, for example, uses 650 pounds of paper every year.

To meet this need, foreign timber companies have purchased giant areas of untouched forest in the Amazon. With better equipment and more workers, these companies can log an area far faster than their counterparts in Brazil, Peru, and other Amazonian nations. Nor are they too concerned with the damage they cause. "They really have one goal," according to forestry expert Bill Laurance, "and that is to extract the maximum amount of timber in the minimum amount of time."[14]

Government permits are required to log in the Amazon. In reality, however, environmental agencies lack the authority to enforce logging regulations. Brazil's environmental protection agency does not have nearly enough officers to patrol an area half the size of the United States. Ninety-four percent of all fines that the officers do impose are thrown out in court. The result is that 80 percent of all logging in the Amazon is done illegally.

Although there are more than seven hundred types of trees in the rain forest, loggers are only interested in the twenty or so species that have commercial value. Mahogany and cedar are particularly precious. A single mahogany tree can be worth as much as twenty thousand dollars. Unfortunately, these trees are rarely concentrated in one part of the forest. Instead, they are spread out over

Finally, Brazil vows to preserve 10% of its ravaged Amazon rain forest

Logging the Underwater Forest

When the reservoir behind the giant Tucuruí dam was filled in the 1980s, millions of healthy trees were covered with water. But the "alligator men" of Tucuruí do not let water stand in the way of their logging operations.

The alligator men earned their nickname for their ability to retrieve logs from far beneath the reservoir's surface. Armed with waterproof chain saws, the loggers dive to the bottom of the reservoir to cut mahogany and other valuable trees. The logs are then floated to the side of the lake, where trucks are waiting to take them off to the sawmills.

many acres, and logging crews must search far and wide for them. Writer Gabrielle Walker describes the loggers' effect on the forest:

> The standard practice is to roam the forest cutting any likely looking trees. As they come crashing down, they pull others with them because they are entangled in a mass of gnarled woody vines, many of them thick as a human arm. . . . Then there's more carnage as a second retrieval team blunders around on a bulldozer until it finds and hauls out the downed trees.[15]

Many of the trees that are cut down have little or no commercial value and are left to rot. Other trees remain standing but are so damaged by bulldozers and other heavy machinery that they eventually die. Researchers have determined that for every tree that is taken out of the rain forest, twenty-seven additional trees are severely damaged, 130 feet of road are created, and more than 6,000 square feet of canopy are destroyed. While the forest can recover from this damage, it is a lengthy process. Logged areas require at least seventy years to return to their original condition.

In the meantime, the logged areas are far more vulnerable to fire. Without the thick protective canopy, the vegetation on the forest floor quickly loses its moisture in the hot sun. A single spark can turn into a raging wild fire. "Fire is becoming more and more common," according to Christopher Uhl, a researcher in the Amazon. "It will increase as landscapes are altered. The high forest is by nature quite resistant to fire, but as soon as you begin to alter it, it is much more prone to burning."[16]

Logging also increases the strain on the forest by allowing more people to enter it. Thousands of families use the roads left behind by loggers to move farther into the forest. The result is more permanent settlements in the Amazon.

Poverty, population, and debt

Eighty percent of the tiny nation of Suriname is covered in Amazonian rain forest. But political instability and civil war in the 1980s ruined Suriname's economy. By the early 1990s, one in five people were unemployed and inflation was skyrocketing.

In 1995 a handful of giant foreign companies presented the government of Suriname with a plan to log 40 percent of the country. Through their logging operations, the companies would invest millions of dollars in the local economy and create thousands of jobs. For the government of a desperately poor nation, it was a difficult offer to refuse.

Suriname's plight highlights one of the biggest factors that drives the destruction of the Amazon. The people of Amazonian nations often live in terrible poverty. Exploding population growth adds to the problem. For example, 165 million people live in Brazil today, but that number will grow to over 200 million early in the next century. Brazil must figure out a way to feed and clothe all of these people.

A settlement in Brazil. As logging companies clear the forests, the empty spaces they leave behind are soon taken over by colonists.

Rates of Destruction

Global

2.47 acres per second: equivalent to two U.S. football fields

150 acres per minute

214,000 acres per day: an area larger than New York City

78 million acres per year: an area larger than Poland

In Brazil

5.4 million acres per year (estimate averaged for period 1979–1990)

6–9 million indigenous people inhabited the Brazilian rain forest in 1500. In 1992, less than 200,000 remained

---

The simplest solution to these problems appears to lie in the resources of the Amazon. The governments hope that they can feed their poor and repay their debts through the development of the rain forest. Where environmentalists see only the destruction of the forest, the governments see an opportunity for economic growth.

The nations that own the Amazon argue that they have the right to use it as they choose. They point out that the United States ravaged many of its own natural resources in the late 1800s, when miners, loggers, and ranchers settled the western frontier. At the same time, the people of the Amazon must be given other ways to earn a living. "Anyone, American, Dutch or whatever, who comes in and tells us not to cut the forest has to give us another way to live," says Rob Sabajo, a native of Suriname. "And so far they haven't done that."[17]

Developing the rain forest is a short-term solution at best. It quickly uses up resources that cannot be replaced. The supply of gold, iron, and timber in the Amazon may appear to be limitless, but it is not. When the resources have been used, the economic and social problems that the Amazonian nations started with will remain.

3

The Price of
Destruction

IN THE FALL of 1997 a cloud of smoke hovered over eight hundred thousand square miles of the Amazon. The smoke was so thick that boats were unable to travel on the Amazon River. Airports closed down dozens of times because pilots could not see well enough to land. In the Brazilian city of Manaus, the sun disappeared from view for days on end. Hospitals reported a 40 percent increase in sickness related to the smoke.

It was burning season in the rain forest. As they do every year from July to November, ranchers and farmers were setting fire to their land to make way for cattle and crops. "Every year things burn," said Antonio de Oliveira, acting superintendent of Brazil's environmental agency, "but this year it's out of control." [18]

The peak rate of deforestation in the Amazon occurred during the burning season of 1987–88. With nearly two-thirds of the Amazon falling within its borders, Brazil suffered the majority of the destruction. The Brazil National Institute for Space Research estimated that one and a half square miles of the Brazilian Amazon were being cleared every hour during the late 1980s. Overall, more than thirteen thousand square miles were disappearing every year. In other Amazonian nations, the loss was nearly as dramatic.

Criticism from environmentalists around the world forced Brazil and other Amazonian nations to take immediate action. Stricter cutting policies were put in place, and hundreds of millions of dollars were spent on rain forest conservation. For a time it seemed as if these efforts were working. By the beginning of the 1990s, the rate of forest loss had fallen to as little as four thousand square miles a year. Amazonian nations claimed victory in the war against deforestation.

The fires of 1997 have proven those claims to be false. "The burning of the Amazon is not over. It's getting worse,"[19] says Stephan Schwartzman, a scientist with the Environmental Defense Fund, a U.S. conservation group. According to information released by the Brazilian government in early 1998, 11,196 square miles of the Amazon were lost during the 1994–95 burning season. An additional 7,000 square miles disappeared between 1995 and 1996.

The rate of destruction may be even higher. Some scientists estimate that for every acre shown as cleared or burned in satellite images, another acre has been destroyed beneath the forest canopy. Taking this hidden damage into account, a study by a Brazilian congressional commission estimates that 22,393 square miles of rain forest are being lost each year.

The exact rate of destruction in the Amazon is the subject of much debate. However, it is clear that the Amazon was relatively untouched before large-scale development began nearly thirty years ago. In that short time, between 12 and 15 percent of the Amazon has been lost due to mining, ranching, farming, and logging. The impact of this destruction is felt by the plants, animals, and people that live in the Amazon. It is also felt by people around the world.

Greenhouse effect

The thousands of fires used to clear the Amazon cause more than just visibility problems. They also release enormous amounts of carbon dioxide into the atmosphere. An average of eighty-eight tons of carbon are released for every acre of tropical forest that is burned.

Carbon dioxide is the primary "greenhouse" gas. When it accumulates in the atmosphere, it forms an invisible shield that blocks escaping heat. This condition is called the greenhouse effect.

With no outlet, the temperature of the atmosphere begins to rise. Recent studies have shown that the atmosphere's temperature has risen by one degree Fahrenheit over the last one hundred years. Some scientists believe that this phenomenon, known as global warming, could have disastrous consequences. If the earth continues to grow warmer, heat waves, violent storms, and droughts could be the result. A significant rise in temperature could melt the polar ice caps, which would cause severe flooding around the world.

Other scientists are less concerned. They argue that the planet's temperature rises and falls naturally over thousands of years. Human activities such as the destruction of

The greenhouse effect.

An Unlikely Fuel Source

Brazilian Indians use oil taken from the co-paiba tree as a skin softener. But it can also be used to power a diesel-engine car. Copaiba oil has properties that are very similar to that of diesel fuel. An acre of these trees can produce as much as twenty-five barrels of this oil every year. Researchers are now experimenting with the tree to determine whether it may someday be able to help replace the world's dwindling supply of fossil fuels.

the rain forest are not to blame for these rises. Nor should the public worry about the consequences of what these scientists believe is a perfectly natural process.

While the debate over global warming continues, the destruction of the rain forest dumps ton after ton of carbon dioxide into the atmosphere. Because of the amount of rain forest burning within its borders, Brazil may be the source of as much as 10 percent of all greenhouse gases. However, automobiles and industrial pollution still produce far more carbon dioxide. The United States is the world's biggest source of greenhouse gases.

Rain forests also affect the amount of carbon dioxide in the atmosphere through their role as a cleaning mechanism. The densely packed trees breathe in large amounts of carbon dioxide and breathe out large amounts of water and oxygen as they make their food. Experts fear that the loss of the trees will cause less carbon dioxide to be absorbed from the atmosphere.

Ecological damage

While the side effects of increased carbon in the atmosphere will be felt around the world, it is just one of many ecological systems that is disturbed by the loss of the rain forest. At the regional level, for example, rain forest destruction upsets the delicate hydrological cycles that control rain. In the Amazon, 50 percent of rainfall is recycled by evapotranspiration—the process that returns rain caught by trees and plants to the atmosphere. Another 25 percent of rainfall is returned to the atmosphere through direct evaporation from leaves.

Without the thick forest canopy, this efficient recycling system breaks down quickly. In areas where the forest has been logged, the amount of rainfall drops tremendously. Long periods of drought are the result. The droughts make it difficult to grow crops and increase the forest's vulnerability to fire.

The thick canopy of a healthy rain forest also forms an umbrella to protect soils from powerful rainstorms. The water that leaks through the canopy is slowed down by its passage through the dense canopy layers. When rain finally reaches the forest floor, the complex root structure of the trees prevents the soil from washing away.

Without a canopy in place, a rainstorm has a different effect. Unchecked by vegetation, rain pounds into the earth, washing the soil into rivers and streams. The loss of soils and their nutrients makes it difficult for new plants to grow in a cleared area. At the same time rivers and streams are muddied, making it difficult for fish to survive. The soil is carried downstream where it clogs the reservoirs behind dams and makes them unusable.

A healthy rain forest also helps prevent flooding. The rain that makes its way through the canopy layers to the ground is absorbed by the complex system of tree roots buried just beneath the surface. The roots release the water slowly and carefully. More is released during times of drought to keep the rivers from drying up. Less water is released during the rainy season to keep the rivers from overflowing. Streams and rivers are far more likely to flood without trees in place to regulate water runoff.

Species loss

In the short term, it may be difficult to measure the effects of rain forest destruction on the amount of rain or the temperature of the earth's atmosphere. But the damage that chain saws and bulldozers inflict on the plants, animals, and insects of the Amazon is very clear. Many of these species cannot be found anywhere else, and the destruction of rain forests is quickly driving them to extinction.

Destruction of habitat is the leading cause of species extinction. When humans cut down the forest, plants, insects, and animals are forced into smaller and smaller areas. As their populations become concentrated, the danger of extinction increases. A species of butterfly that is found only on a few square acres of the Bolivian Amazon could easily be wiped out by logging, a fire, or by a family trying to clear land for a farm.

Human encroachment poses another threat to rain forest species. More settlers in the Amazon mean more people hunting for food. In Ecuador's rain forest, the discovery of oil has brought development and thousands of settlers. Woolly, howler, and spider monkeys, once hidden in the depths of the forest, are now surrounded by hungry people. Many monkeys end up on dinner tables because there is little else for the settlers to eat.

The black caiman often meets the same fate. The caiman, a relative of the alligator, can grow to over thirteen feet in length. Originally it was prized by hunters for its valuable skin. So many were lost that the black caiman was declared an endangered species and protected by law. Even so, hunters continue to kill them for their skins and for food. Caiman meat, well-salted so that it will not spoil, is sold in the markets of Brazil and Colombia.

Black spider monkeys are just one of the species of primates threatened by hungry settlers who have nothing else to eat.

Unknown numbers

No one knows exactly how many species are lost for every acre of the Amazon that is logged. Since the eighteenth century, when the biologist Linnaeus created the classification system used by scientists today, approximately 1.5 million living species have been identified around the world.

This is just a small percentage of the number of species worldwide that actually exist. Estimates for the number of species that remain to be discovered vary widely, from a minimum of 1.5 million to as many as 30 million. Michael Smith, a scientist with the Center for Marine Conservation, says that the exact number of species waiting to be identified is not important: "What is important is that the number still to be discovered is greater than the number we've been able to process in the 250 years since Linneaus."[20]

Half of the species that scientists have classified were found in the Amazon and other tropical rain forests. Deforestation is rapidly taking its toll in these areas. One study estimates that twenty-seven thousand species are lost each year in the world's rain forests alone. "You're talking about the potential loss of a quarter to half of all species on earth,"[21] warns biologist Thomas Lovejoy.

Extinction is a part of the natural world. Species are constantly dying out while others take their place. It is the rate of extinction in the Amazon that is both unusual and troublesome. Scientists do not know what will result from the rapid extinction of such a large number of species. They do know that the disappearance of species unique to the Amazon rain forest could deprive human beings of an invaluable resource.

Medicine

Modern medicine depends heavily on the rain forest. One-fourth of the medicines used in the United States and other countries come from rain forest plants. Seventy percent of the plant species that are effective in fighting cancer were discovered in tropical rain forests. An acre of Amazon rain forest might hold the cure for AIDS, cancer, or other deadly diseases.

One of the most important medicines to come out of the Amazon is curare. Made from a particular kind of liana, early explorers in the Amazon found natives using it on the tips of their arrows. Arrows tipped with curare paralyzed the animals they struck, making it easier to hunt in the thick vegetation.

Today, doctors use curare to perform complex heart surgery. Injected into a patient, it relaxes muscles and allows the doctor to operate. Only recently have attempts to manufacture curare in laboratories been successful.

Quinine is another valuable rain forest medicine. European travelers first encountered it in use by the Incas in seventeenth-century Peru. Extracted from the boiled bark of a cinchona tree, it is an effective treatment for malaria, a crippling tropical disease that affects millions of people around the world.

As deforestation ravages the Amazon, scientists have realized that they need to act quickly. Thousands of researchers are now combing the forest with hopes of finding beneficial plants. Still, fewer than 1 percent of the 250,000 known tropical plants have been analyzed. Mark Plotkin, a scientist who assesses the medicinal potential of plants in the Amazon, believes that scientists are missing potential benefits even in plants they have had a chance to study: "I really do believe that laboratory tests just don't always do it—that we're missing miracle drugs right and left."[22]

Ethnobotany

One of the best ways to pinpoint important plants quickly is through ethnobotany—the study of how people who live in the rain forest use the plants around them. Ethnobotanists conduct thorough interviews and observe the forest people closely, hoping to learn their secrets. Native people use over thirteen hundred plant species to relieve aches and pains, cure infections, and treat snake bites.

The key to this wealth of knowledge is each tribe's shaman. The shaman acts as the village doctor, using these plants to treat a variety of ailments. His expertise has been passed down through countless generations and cannot be

Curare-tipped darts such as these are used by natives in their hunt for prey. A muscle-relaxant, curare is also used in modern-day heart surgery.

A village shaman, or medicine man, looks over his crop of curative plants. Ethnobotanists have catalogued over thirteen hundred different plant species used by shamans to treat injuries, ease pain, and cure disease.

found in any book or laboratory. "Each time a medicine man dies," says Plotkin, "it is like an irreplaceable library burning down."[23]

People of the forest

Plotkin and other ethnobotanists have reason to worry about the disappearance of shamans. As loggers, miners, farmers, and ranchers cut into the Amazon, they are destroying land that has been inhabited by native cultures for thousands of years.

At one time there were as many as 10 million tribal people living in the Amazon. Today, only 200,000 remain. Since the beginning of this century, Amazonian tribes have been wiped out by disease and violence at the rate of almost 1 per year.

While there are many explanations for this tragedy, each is directly linked to the economic development of the Amazon. Giant dams have flooded tribal lands. Outsiders are moving into native territories in their search for gold, timber, and other riches. Settlers are converting the forest that native people depend on for survival into pasture for cattle.

The settlers also carry with them diseases that are deadly to tribal people. Measles, tuberculosis, whooping cough, and influenza are common in the rest of the world, where people have built up natural defenses, or are immunized, against them. Amazonian natives have never been exposed to these diseases. As a result, their first contact is often fatal.

 ## Searching for the Next Wonder Drug

The scientists and drug companies combing the rain forest for new drugs are motivated in part by the story of rosy periwinkle. Thirty-five years ago, children with leukemia had only a 20 percent chance of survival, and people suffering from Hodgkin's disease faced almost certain death. But rosy periwinkle, a plant found in the rain forests of Madagascar, brought new hope to victims of these diseases. Drugs made from this plant give childhood leukemia patients an 80 percent chance of recovery and have dramatically improved the chances for Hodgkin's patients as well. Scientists are now searching the Amazon for plants that may be as valuable to medicine as the rosy periwinkle.

Cat's claw, made from the bark of a rain forest plant, just might be the next great discovery. Peruvian Indians have used it as a medicine for centuries. In a January 1997 *Prevention* article, Varro Tyler, an expert on plant and herbal medicine, is cautiously optimistic: "It needs a lot of work to prove its benefits, but it's potentially the most important new botanical discovery of recent times."

Drugs made from the rosy periwinkle are most effective in the treatment of childhood leukemia and Hodgkin's disease.

Thousands more have been killed by settlers who want to claim the land as their own. One investigation of the treatment of native people in Brazil uncovered a long list of atrocities, including the massacre of whole tribes using machine guns, poison, and explosives.

The Yanomami and Kayapó tribes

When a tribe is wiped out, an entire culture is lost. Unique languages, beliefs, and customs disappear forever. Also lost is the tribe's special knowledge of the rain forest. Tribes like the Yanomami provide outsiders with a model for how to live in harmony with the rain forest. Experience has taught the Yanomami how to survive in the environment that surrounds them. They grow crops without destroying huge amounts of forest. They gather medicines from plants and hunt animals for food. The forest is also vital to their religious and spiritual beliefs. Their culture cannot survive anywhere but in the forest.

The Yanomami once roamed freely across thousands of square miles of southern Venezuela and northern Brazil. Unfortunately, settlers are pouring into the territory that the Yanomami formerly called their own. In 1987 a gold rush brought forty thousand miners to the traditional Yanomami lands. The effect was devastating. Fifteen hundred of the ten thousand Yanomami in the region died in just three years, victims of malaria, tuberculosis, and malnutrition. The Brazilian military finally removed most of the miners, but the damage had already been done. "They gave us rice and wheat, but then we got sick," says one Yanomami of the miners. "They pretended to be our friends, but they are killing us."[24]

Another tribe that suffers as settlers move in is the Kayapó Indians. At the beginning of this century, thirty thousand Kayapó lived in the Amazonian forests. Now less than four thousand members of this once-dominant tribe remain. Pneumonia, hepatitis, and malaria have devastated their villages. Violent conflicts over land with miners, ranchers, and loggers are common and have resulted in many deaths.

A social worker helps a Yanomami Indian and her baby. Lacking natural immunity and medical treatment, most native populations have been decimated by diseases such as malaria and tuberculosis brought in by miners and other outsiders.

In recent years the Kayapó have waged a bitter public battle for survival. They have organized demonstrations in Brasília to protest the dumping of radioactive waste in their territory and the lack of rights for native people in the Brazilian constitution. Several Kayapó leaders made the long trip to Washington, D.C., to fight—successfully on this occasion—against a proposed system of dams that would have flooded much of their land.

As fiercely as the Kayapó defend their culture and land, many tribe members also want to enjoy the benefits of modern society. Some Kayapó chiefs allow logging and mining on their lands in exchange for a percentage of the profits. This newfound wealth has brought pickup trucks, televisions, and electricity to their villages.

The Kayapó may be able to adapt to modern society and the loss of their land, but their culture will probably not survive the transition. "I think that in 20 years, most Indians will be growing up in slums on the edges of our cities," says Francisco de Oliviera Ramos, an administrator for Brazil's agency of Indian affairs. "I don't want to live to see it. A Kayapo warrior in a city is a very sad sight."[25]

Food

The loss of the rain forest may also be a loss for food lovers around the world. Many of the most familiar foods in the United States and Europe have their origins in the Amazon rain forest. One notable example, chocolate, comes from the beans of the cacao plant of the Amazon. Tomatoes and papaya were first discovered on the vines of the Amazon.

The majority of these popular foods are now grown on farms in other parts of the world. But as the case of the manioc, or cassava, demonstrates, its continued survival in the Amazon is very important. In the United States maniocs are usually found in Latin markets or in the form of tapioca pudding. Worldwide, however, the manioc tree provides food for 300 million people. The starchy roots of the manioc are boiled and eaten like potatoes, turned into flour, or even used to make beer.

In the 1930s a disease struck farms and threatened to destroy the world's supply of manioc. Scientists returned to the Amazon to find wild varieties of manioc that were resistant to disease. These resistant plants were then mixed with farm-grown or domesticated manioc. In this way, a food staple for millions was saved.

Wild plants continue to be used to improve the fruits and vegetables sold in grocery stores. Tomatoes from the rain forests of Peru and Ecuador have been bred with the domesticated variety to make tomatoes in the United States more colorful and nutritious. Wild peanuts have been used to improve domesticated peanuts' ability to fight off pests and disease. Scientists also draw on the genes of wild plants to create crops that grow faster, and under more difficult conditions, than ever before. These new strains could be the key to creating a supply of protein-rich food for impoverished countries.

Hundreds of other fruits and vegetables from the Amazon could find their way into the world's supermarkets. One species of palm tree bears a red fruit that contains one of the highest concentrations of vitamin A in the plant kingdom. The camu camu, a small member of the guava family, is loaded with vitamin C. The naranjilla, a fruit that tastes like a blend of a strawberry and pineapple, can already be found on the breakfast table of some Ecuadoran families. According to Michael Balick, a botanist with the New York Botanical Garden, current use of rain forest plants "represents only the tip of a huge beneficial iceberg of possibilities."[26]

Destroying the unknown

The most alarming aspect of the destruction of the Amazon is that no one knows what is being lost. Knowledge of

Chocolate in Trouble?

A recent edition of the *New York Times* contained alarming news for the millions of chocolate lovers around the world. "Chocoholics Take Note: Beloved Bean in Peril," warned a front-page headline.

Chocolate is manufactured by mixing sugar and water with the roasted beans of the cacao tree. For reasons that are not clear to scientists, the cacao tree is extremely vulnerable to insects and disease. A shortage of the trees, coupled with a rising demand for chocolate worldwide, threatens to send the price of a candy bar sky-high.

To combat this threat, conservationists recently met with representatives from the Mars, Cadbury, Nestlé, and Hershey companies. The purpose of this unusual gathering was to develop strategies for growing disease- and pest-free cacao trees. Says Carol Knight of the American Cocoa Research Institute in a May 4, 1998, *New York Times* article, "We have to figure out a way to grow it [the cacao] sustainably. Nobody wants to lose chocolate."

These cacao beans will soon be ready for harvesting, roasting, and processing into cocoa.

Taming a Toxic Root

Today, the manioc plant provides food to hundreds of millions of people around the world, but the first person to taste it very likely ended up dead. In addition to an abundance of carbohydrates, the roots of the manioc tree also contain a deadly poison called cyanide.

The Tikuna Indians of Brazil learned long ago how to avoid the deadly taste of cyanide. A careful preparation process allows them to eat the vegetable and survive. First, the manioc is pounded into a pulp. The poison is then squeezed out. The final step is to heat the pulp to remove all traces of cyanide.

Today, the Tikuna grow more than one hundred types of manioc. Each one has a unique feature, whether it is size, taste, the ability to grow in a certain type of soil, or a resistance to a particular disease.

how the Amazon works, and what lives within its borders, is very limited. The lack of knowledge about the rain forest makes clearing it even riskier.

This risk is not easily reduced. The interdependence of species means that logging in one area can have far-reaching and unexpected effects. As authors Robert Goodland and Howard Irwin write,

> A certain species of plant may not in itself be of recognized economic importance to man, but it may provide the food for an insect species which at another time of year pollinates the flowers of a tree of importance. . . . Until more is known . . . about the balance of nature within the forest, it is courting disaster to cut over large areas.[27]

Humans continue to court disaster. As millions of acres of forest disappear, humanity may be destroying a plant that can supply food to millions of people, cure AIDS, or even fill the gas tanks of automobiles. We may be losing solutions that we could never dream up on our own.

4

The Fight for
the Forest

IN 1974 A single forest fire raged across thirty-nine hundred square miles of the Brazilian Amazon. It burned for weeks and was the largest man-made fire in history. News of the fire spread around the world, carrying with it the growing realization that even an area as large as the Amazon could be destroyed by careless human activities.

In the 1980s and 1990s the concern over deforestation in the Amazon has increased even further. In part the concern is due to a flood of news reports about logging, mining, and the plight of native tribes. Worldwide there has also been a growing awareness of the importance of environmental protection. The conservation movement has gathered tremendous momentum over the past twenty-five years. Deforestation, recycling, energy use, and pollution are now important issues in the lives of everyone from schoolchildren to political leaders.

With increased awareness and concern have come countless plans to save the Amazon rain forest. Conservation organizations, concerned citizens, governments, and rock stars have taken up the cause. Millions of dollars have poured into conservation efforts, and thousands of projects have been launched. Many of these efforts have been unsuccessful. According to Stephan Schwartzman of the Environmental Defense Fund, "Deforestation has done nothing but go up. Where the most money has gone is where the fires have increased the most."[28]

An Indian woman plants banana seeds in a small clearing near her home. Most rain forest natives are able to farm the land without destroying it, a practice known as sustainable use.

To make their projects more effective, many conservationists are heeding the lessons of those who have lived in the forest for thousands of years. Indian tribes and others use the rain forest as home, supermarket, and drug store. Yet they cause little damage to the rain forest. According to Tom Melham, a senior writer for the National Geograhic Society, "such groups have benefited continuously from their environment without eliminating it. In contrast, modern man—armed with all his more powerful technology— has been far more destructive."[29] The idea that humans can use natural resources like the Amazon without destroying them is called sustainable use. This strategy is a critical part of many current efforts to save the Amazon.

Learning from the forest people

Forest tribes such as the Kayapó and Yanomami have been farming the Amazon successfully for hundreds of

years. One technique the tribes use is called shifting cultivation. The process begins when a family clears a small
area of forest and then plants a crop. The ashes of the
cleared trees are used as a fertilizer to add nutrients to
the soil.

With the first crop in the ground, the family then plants
a series of crops in other small clearings. After several
years of farming the first clearing, the family plants trees
there, and allows it to grow back into rain forest. Mean-
while, the other clearings continue to produce food. Like
the first clearing, they are allowed time to replenish their
soils when their productivity drops. Twenty years later the
rain forest is healed and the family can begin to use the
first field again.

Successful shifting cultivation requires tremendous
knowledge of the forest. The Kayapó carefully divide their
land into zones based on the type of trees, soils, and vegetation and the presence of water and hills. They use more
than six hundred plant species. Amazingly, some Kayapó
can identify hundred of trees simply by smell.

The Kayapó also have a remarkable understanding of
the interdependence of species. They realize that some
plant species grow best when planted together. They de-
scribe these species as "good friends" or "good neighbors."
By planting a well-chosen blend of species and cultivating
them carefully, the Kayapó create forest gardens that are as
rich in plant and animal life as an untouched area of rain
forest. The ground beneath these gardens is actually richer
in nutrients than ordinary Amazonian soils.

Agroforestry

The forest gardens of the Kayapó also demonstrate a
sustainable farming technique called agroforestry. Agroforestry is an attempt to mimic the structure and diversity
of a natural forest. Both food crops and wild species of
trees are planted in a cleared area. In a few years the first
crop is harvested. The trees continue to grow, bearing useful fruits, nuts, and medicines in the process. Their
canopies and roots protect the nutrients of the soil. Other

crops that can grow in the shade are planted. After several decades the clearing is healthy and ready to be used again.

Like shifting cultivation, agroforestry is an ancient approach to farming. For generations the Mayaruna and Remo tribes grew aguaje trees in small forest gardens deep in the Peruvian Amazon. The trees provided them with a delicious and valuable fruit that is now used to flavor drinks and ice cream. At the same time the trees helped preserve the nutrients in the soil. A single plot could be farmed for twenty years or more.

More recently, the Peruvian government encouraged the tribes to grow corn and raise cattle. The government hoped that these crops would be more profitable than traditional crops. However, these uses of the rain forest ruined soils and increased the need for land. The traditional methods of

 Pest Control in the Amazon

The native people of the Amazon rely on ancient methods of farming to produce rich and sustainable crops. They have even developed ways to prevent insects from eating their crops. For example, the Kayapó place Aztec ants in their gardens when leaf-cutter ants are threatening. They know from experience that, while the Aztec ants will not harm the crops, they possess an odor that will drive the leaf-cutter ants away.

This simple technique could benefit pest control efforts in other countries. By one estimate, insects destroy 40 percent of all food grown each year. Farmers use ton after ton of synthetic pesticides to protect their crops, but nothing works for long. The insects quickly build up a resistance to the pesticide, and the chemicals end up polluting rivers and streams.

The Kayapó method has already been put to use in the United States. Some citrus farmers in Florida protect their crops by introducing one type of insect that feeds on the threatening pest. The farmers get effective pest control without relying on dangerous and costly chemicals.

cultivation were forgotten, and the forest suffered. "It was a lose-lose situation," says Jim Penn of the Rainforest Conservation Foundation. "Every year people worked harder and harder to further extinguish a valuable resource."[30]

The Rainforest Conservation Foundation is now working with local farmers to change this situation. Aguaje trees have again been planted in forest gardens, and traditional farming methods are again in use. The rain forest has benefited, and the people are once again in control of the health of their land. "If we don't protect our resources, who's going to do it?"[31] asks forest-dweller Raul Huanaquiri.

Agroforestry and shifting cultivation do not eliminate the need to clear more of the forest. However, they are more efficient ways of using the land. Land can be farmed for a longer period of time, and it recovers more quickly so that it can be used again. While farmers who use these techniques still have to clear the forest, they do so in much smaller amounts.

Lacking the same skills and knowledge, settlers who moved to the Amazon in the last thirty years have been unable to farm successfully for any length of time. Their failure on one plot of land forces them to clear another and try again. The result is widespread destruction of the forest.

To collect latex, a milky-white juice used to produce rubber, tappers cut into the tree's bark and attach a cup below the incision. This method does no harm to the tree and allows for repeated harvests.

Rubber tappers

Rubber tappers have lived in the Amazon for only a fraction of the time that Indians have, but they too know how to survive in the rain forest without destroying it. Rubber tappers, or *seringuieros* as they are called in Brazil, use machetes to slash the bark of wild rubber trees. The slash allows latex to flow out of the tree and into a cup but does not kill the tree. Latex is turned into large balls of rubber that are sold at market. The rubber becomes part of tires, airplanes, raincoats, and countless other products around the world.

An estimated five hundred thousand rubber tappers live and work in the Amazon rain forest, using the same trees year after year. During the rainy season they harvest Brazil nuts to sell. Other workers gather palm hearts, oils, and other products that are valuable commercially.

The biggest threat to the rubber tappers' livelihood comes from others seeking to use the Amazon's resources. Ranchers and loggers, eager to clear the rain forest, have continually pushed rubber tappers off their land, often at the point of a gun. Beginning in the 1970s, a young rubber tapper named Chico Mendes led the resistance against the land-grabbers. He organized *empates*, or standoffs, in which men, women, and children would join hands and protect their land from chain saw–wielding ranchers. Unable to cut the trees without harming innocent people, the ranchers were turned away.

Chico Mendes, a rubber tapper who led the resistance against land-grabbing ranchers and loggers, was killed in 1988 by opponents of his conservationist efforts.

Extractive reserves

The rubber tappers' land continued to be destroyed in spite of the *empates*. The forest people needed a more permanent solution. In 1985 the rubber tappers produced a paper that stated: "We demand a development policy for the Amazon that addresses the needs of rubber tappers and respects our rights."[32] International conservation organizations took up the cause, increasing the pressure on Amazonian governments. Brazil finally acted to protect the rubber tappers and their land by establishing extractive reserves.

An extractive reserve is an area that has been set aside by the government for local people to harvest rain forest products such as latex, coconut oil, palm hearts, and Brazil nuts. The land has legal protection from logging, mining, farming, and other potentially harmful uses. Dozens of extractive reserves covering millions of acres have been established in the Amazon.

Chico Mendes did not live to see his dream realized. He was shot and killed in 1988 by ranchers who were angered by his attempts to stop them from cutting the forest. In his memory, the Brazilian government established the 2.3-million-acre Chico Mendes Extractive Reserve. The average rubber tapper on the reserve collects about eleven hundred pounds of rubber each year. Together, the 250 workers on the Mendes reserve collect about seventy tons of rubber every year.

Giant plantations and low prices

The collection of wild rubber is not an ideal solution to the problem of sustainable development. Rubber tappers on the Mendes reserve cannot compete with the giant plantations where rubber trees are packed closely together. A worker on a rubber plantation may harvest ten times as much rubber as harvesters of wild rubber. One day's production of rubber at the Michelin plantation will equal a year's supply of rubber from the Mendes reserve.

The giant plantations produce so much rubber that the prices remain low. As a result, wild rubber tappers earn little in return for their hard work. The workers receive as little as 23 cents per pound of rubber collected—just $250 in an entire year.

Despite these difficulties, extractive reserves can be effective conservation tools. Their greatest strength is that they give people a reason to preserve the land. If they take care of the land and keep it healthy, it will continue to support them; if they destroy it, their source of income will disappear forever.

Research supports the idea that a forest managed for rubber and other sustainable resources is more valuable over time than one that is logged or otherwise destroyed. A study in Peru found that a small plot of land would produce a one-time profit of $1,000 if it was logged. The same plot of land contained seventy-two plant products, including latex, that could be harvested by local people and sold. The harvest of these products would bring a profit of $422 every year. "You want development to be sustainable for the ecosystem," says Glenn Prickett of the Natural Resources Defense Council, an environmental group based in New York. "If you destroy the forest, you get short-term income, but you've lost a long-term resource."[33]

Ecotourism

Ecotourism represents another way that the Amazon can provide economic benefits to the nations that own it without being destroyed by logging, mining, ranching, or farming. Ecotourists are the millions of people who visit national parks and forests around the world every year. They are motivated by their desire to experience nature firsthand.

The money that these travelers spend on their trips—for food, lodging, tours, and souvenirs—is a tremendous boost to local economies. The hope is that this new industry will reduce the need for more forest destruction. Giving the inhabitants of an Amazonian village a way to make money besides logging or farming can reduce the destructive pressure on the rain forest.

One of the best examples of how ecotourism and conservation can work hand in hand is found outside of the Amazon, in Costa Rica. Twenty-seven percent of this small Central American nation is protected by law. The national parks safeguard the rain forest and all the species that live in it.

As a result of these conservation efforts, Costa Rica has seen a dramatic increase in tourism. Hundreds of thousands of people visit the country each year eager to witness its natural beauty. The millions of dollars that ecotourists spend on food, lodging, and other services help boost the nation's economy.

Amazonian nations are now trying to imitate Costa Rica's success on their own lands. The Indians of San Jos are hoping that ecotourism will help save their traditional lands in northwest Bolivia. The lands are threatened by

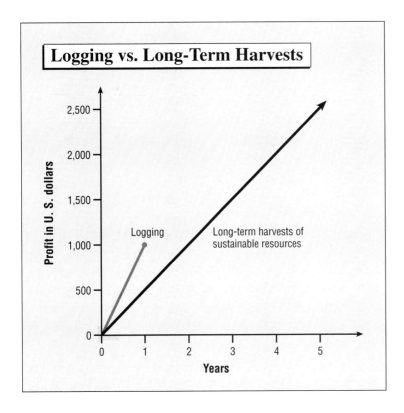

Logging vs. Long-Term Harvests

Logging

Long-term harvests of sustainable resources

Profit in U. S. dollars

Years

loggers searching for mahogany and by oil exploration less than twenty miles away.

With the help of conservation groups, the people of San Jos are building small lodges and nature trails. They hope that their beautiful forest, and the jaguars, toucans, and monkeys that live in it, will attract a small part of the $250 billion spent every year on ecotourism around the world.

For this venture to be successful, it must have the full support of the Bolivian government. The government has the power to allow oil or logging companies onto the land at any time. However, if it can be convinced that the land is more economically valuable as an ecotourism reserve, it will be far more likely to spare the land from more destructive forms of economic development.

Peru's experience with ecotourism highlights some of the risks involved. The Cuzco-Amazónico Lodge in Peru was receiving more than three thousand visitors each year by 1990. The lodge generated enough income to pay for

Tourists pause on a guided hike through the rain forest. Properly controlled, ecotourism can be an environmentally friendly alternative to logging, mining, and ranching, as well as a means of generating income for poor Amazon nations.

the protection and maintenance of a large nature reserve. Many local people were also employed by the operation.

A poor economy worldwide, as well as safety concerns within Peru's borders, drove the number of visitors to the country down by 75 percent in the 1990s. No matter how beautiful the rain forest may be, people will not visit if they fear for their safety or if they are faring poorly economically.

Ecotourism can also pose risks to the rain forest it is designed to protect. Too many visitors in a natural area can be harmful. The noise that ecotourists make can drive away wildlife, and the garbage they produce can spoil a natural area. Visitors could venture off a trail and accidentally destroy the home of an insect or butterfly.

Another concern is that ecotourists will harm native cultures. Visitors from the United States and Europe bring their own values, customs, and merchandise to the rain forest. It is possible that native people will adopt some of these ways and lose part of their traditional culture.

When properly done, however, ecotourism promotes conservation of the rain forest in several ways. On a local level, it encourages native people to preserve a specific piece of land, as the people of San Jos have done. It can also encourage conservation on a national level. When governments recognize that the rain forest can attract millions of visitors—and the dollars they spend—they become more interested in preserving it. Successful ecotourism requires a basic shift in the way that governments use their natural resource. They must be willing to forego the short-term profits that mining and logging may bring in favor of rewards that will be reaped over a longer period of time.

People and parks

If ecotourists, rubber tappers, settlers, and forest people are to use the land in a sustainable way, they must be assured that the land they are caring for belongs to them and will not be invaded by loggers, ranchers, and miners. Uncertain land ownership has plagued settlers and native people in the Amazon. According to the anthropologist Charles Wagley, "The problem of land titles probably causes as much human misery as anything in Amazonia."[34]

This misery is felt by the forest as well. A farmer has little incentive to care for the land today if he thinks that it could very well be stolen away tomorrow. The careful

Rain forest lodges such as this one provide safe havens for ecotourists but can also threaten the lifestyle and customs of natives living nearby.

planning and work that goes into successful shifting cultivation or agroforestry can be ruined in a minute by a chain
saw–wielding invader who wants to make a short-term
profit by logging that same land.

Extractive reserves are one way that Amazonian nations
have responded to this problem. The creation of national
parks is another. Ecuador has led the way with the creation
of the Yasuní National Park. Covering six thousand square
miles near Ecuador's border with Colombia and Peru, the
purpose of the park is to protect one of the most diverse areas on earth.

Extractive reserves and parks must take care of both
people and the resource. As Dagmar Werner, a German biologist, says,

> When you talk of saving the rain forests, there are two things
> you should keep in mind. One: Protection of the forest by it-
> self usually doesn't work. Putting fences around rain forests
> and calling them parks is almost certain to fail, largely be-
> cause of the second thing you should keep in mind: People
> are hungry.[35]

People are indeed hungry in the Amazon, and to these
people, national parks like Yasuní represent a source of
income, food, and medicine. Poor settlers slip easily into
the parks to farm or log. Their motive is not to destroy the
rain forest; they simply want to feed themselves and their
families.

National parks in the United States would not be nearly
so well preserved if they were surrounded by thousands of
poor, hungry people. Fences, guards, and millions of dollars are needed to protect parks in the Amazon. This is
money that the governments either do not have or are not
willing to spend on conservation. As a result, Yasuní National Park, as enormous as it is, has only two guards to
protect it.

Governments are hungry, too. They are eager to reap the
economic rewards of the Amazon, even if it means destroying their own national parks. Even Yasuní is vulnerable. The vast reserves of oil hidden under its soil make it a
prime target for development.

Logging

While some environmentalists are pushing for a ban on logging in the rain forest, it is probably not a realistic goal. The wood in the Amazon is simply too valuable, and the countries that own it too poor, to stop cutting. There are better ways to cut the timber, however. It is possible to log in the Amazon without causing quite so much damage.

A research organization called the Amazon Institute of Man and the Environment (IMAZON) has studied sustainable logging methods on plots deep in the heart of the rain forest. Some of the solutions they developed were quite simple. Before chopping down a mahogany tree, for example, the researchers cut the vines attached to it and allowed them to wither. As a result, the mahogany tree was much less likely to pull down other trees when it was cut.

IMAZON researchers also tried to minimize the damage caused by bulldozers as they move through the forest to retrieve felled trees. Their solution was to carefully map the location and type of all the trees in a forest plot. Using this map, they designed a route for the bulldozer that would take it to all the downed trees in the most direct way possible. The result was a logging operation that was less destructive to the other trees in the forest.

The forest plot will also recover more quickly from its wounds. Chris Uhl, an ecologist with IMAZON, claims, "With these practices, you'll be able to go back to the site in 35 years or so for the second harvest."[36] While 35 years may seem like a long time, without these logging techniques it would take the forest more than 70 years to recover.

In Peru researchers are attempting to log the forest in a way that imitates natural growth. Small strips of the forest are cut, creating gaps similar to those left when trees fall naturally. Small branches and leaves are also left behind. They provide nutrients to the forest as it works to heal itself. Horses and other farm animals are used to remove the cut trees, a method that is far less destructive and much more cost effective than using bulldozers.

The biggest challenge for IMAZON and other groups is to convince loggers that they should use these new logging

A Removable Road

Every development project in the Amazon depends on a road to ferry materials to and from the site. The roads do their own damage, though, tearing through the rain forest and displacing wildlife. Is there a better way to build a road?

The Maxus Oil Company thinks so. To service their oil wells in the Ecuadoran Amazon, Maxus has built a new kind of road designed to minimize impact on the forest. The first layer of the road is a carpet made from synthetic fiber designed to protect the soil. Gravel is then laid down on top of the road to form the driving surface.

The most amazing part of the road is that it is removable. When Maxus's oil operations are complete several decades from now, the gravel will be trucked out and the carpet rolled up to use again. The forest will then reclaim the area once used by dump trucks and heavy machinery.

Roads such as this one will remain long after the trucks have gone. Removable roads will allow the forest to reclaim the land.

techniques. This is no easy task. Because loggers will not see the benefits for decades, they are often reluctant to try the improved techniques.

Some advocates for the Amazon argue that the best way to save the forest is to make it off limits to development. But as Charles Wagley notes, "For good or bad, you're not going to keep development out. . . . That's just not realistic."[37] If he is correct, the challenge for conservationists is to minimize the impact that each development project has on the rain forest. As scientists, researchers, and native people have shown, sustainable use of the rain forest is possible. Farming, logging, and mining techniques that are less harmful to the environment do exist.

Governments and conservation groups are now trying to ensure that these techniques are used by as many people as possible, in as many different projects as possible. Researchers like Eric Fernandes of Cornell University are hopeful that sustainable use can work in the Amazon: "I really think you can have people living in harmony with the forest. It's not preservation in the sense that you lock it all up and throw away the key. It's how you use what's there, and manage it, and go with the system."[38]

5

Global Solutions

WHILE IT IS easy to blame the Amazonian nations for the demise of the rain forest, they are not the only ones responsible for its destruction. Asia, Europe, and the United States must also accept a large part of the blame. The demand in these countries for tropical woods, gold, oil, and other products is what drives much of the deforestation. They are home to the stores, malls, and markets where many rain forest products are bought and sold.

The most valuable tree species in the Amazon, mahogany, provides a perfect example of the connection between consumer demand and rain forest loss. Mahogany is prized in the United States and Japan for its beauty and strength. Buyers of cabinets and furniture are willing to pay high prices for products made with this type of wood. The tremendous demand for mahogany, and the high prices that it commands, motivate loggers in the Amazon to search far and wide for the trees. The destruction does not end even when the mahogany tree is removed. The logging of mahogany requires the creation of roads, which, in turn, open up the forest to the logging of other tree species, agriculture, and other destructive uses.

Consumer demand can play an equally important role in slowing rain forest destruction. Consumers encourage conservation of the Amazon simply by using rain forest products that are harvested in a sustainable way. Sustainable products like Brazil nuts require eager buyers in the United States and elsewhere. Without these buyers, Amazonian people would be unable to profit from the harvest of Brazil nuts. Inevitably, they would be forced to turn to logging, farming, or mining simply to survive.

Just as consumer choice is critical to the survival of the Amazon, so are the choices that foreign corporations and governments make. An oil company may elect to use a new technology to construct a pipeline in order to minimize the harm to the rain forest. A foreign bank may decide against loaning money to a project in the Amazon that it believes will cause too much environmental damage. Ultimately, responsible choices by foreign governments, corporations, and consumers will play a major role in conserving the Amazon.

Consumers for conservation?

At times it seems as if the fight to save the Amazon has spilled over into the local grocery store or the cosmetics section of major department stores. Hundreds of products, from lipstick to chocolate bars, are now being sold in the United States and Europe with labels and packaging bearing promises that they will help save the rain forest. Many of the products are made from Amazonian plants. Some companies pledge to donate a percentage of the profits of each item sold to rain forest conservation efforts.

As long as there is demand for the natural resources found in the rain forest, destructive operations such as this gold mine will continue to devastate the area.

Cultural Survival is a nonprofit organization that purchases Amazonian crops harvested without harming the rain forest. It then sells the crops to companies that use them in their products. A percentage of the proceeds from the sales are returned to the native people who were responsible for the harvest.

Ben and Jerry's was one of the first companies to take advantage of this service. Anyone who eats Rainforest

Crunch ice cream bites into Brazil nuts that were harvested in the Amazon and brought to the United States by Cultural Survival.

Many other companies have policies that encourage the protection of the Amazon. The Aveda cosmetics company works with the Yawanawa Indians to obtain materials for its lipsticks and hair care products. Similarly, the Kayapó Indians supply another company, the Body Shop, with Brazil-nut oil for its line of shampoos and conditioners.

Marketing the rain forest

Brazil's environmental agency, the Brazilian Institute for the Environment and Renewable Natural Resources (IBAMA), is also trying to make the connection between people's buying habits and rain forest conservation. IBAMA is establishing a "green label" program to tell consumers if the Amazon products they are purchasing are made in a way that does not harm the forest. These marketing efforts highlight the close relationship between what people in the United States, Europe, and Asia purchase and the destruction of the rain forest.

Separating responsible business behavior from a clever marketing campaign can be a difficult task, however. Critics believe that many corporations are taking advantage of the growing concern for the Amazon to sell their products. They argue that this type of advertising tricks consumers into buying a certain product in the mistaken belief that they are helping to save the rain forest.

It can also be difficult to tell whether rain forest–friendly products are helping to slow destruction in the Amazon. Donations pledged to rain forest conservation do not always reach their intended target. But many of the companies continue to use and market sustainable rain

Ben Cohen and Jerry Greenfield (pictured) were among the first to work with Cultural Survival, a nonprofit organization that helps protect native people of the Amazon.

More Side Effects of Drilling for Oil

Florinda Aylia is an Ecuadoran farmer who must live with the mess that oil companies leave behind. A toxic pit of crude oil half as long as a football field lies right next to her home. The pit has poisoned many of her farm animals and poses a great danger to her family. "You have to always be watching the children," she says in a December 15, 1996, *Houston Chronicle* article. "You have to worry they are going to fall in here. There are a lot of illnesses, and every doctor who comes to see what is happening says it is because of the pit." The high level of oil-related pollution in the water supply has been blamed for cancer, blindness, and other illnesses afflicting the local people.

forest products with the best intentions. "Business is the most powerful tool in the world," says Ben Cohen, co-founder of Ben and Jerry's. "You can either use that tool to oppress people and destroy the environment, or you can use it to liberate people and preserve the environment." [39]

Adds Kate Priest of Emerald Forest, a maker of beauty supplies that donates part of its profits to rain forest conservation, "We're trying to create a new, workable business ethic. I would not be doing this if I thought I was just making shampoo." [40]

Big business

For decades large corporations have profited from the Amazon with little concern for the health of the forest. A seemingly endless amount of land stretched out before the companies, and Amazonian nations were unwilling or unable to govern their activities. They took advantage of these circumstances to log, mine, or drill for oil in the quickest way possible. A messy trail of toxic chemicals, polluted streams, and damaged forests was left behind.

Environmentalists have put enormous pressure on these corporations to improve their environmental record in the Amazon. They want these companies to strengthen their environmental policies and use the most environmentally friendly technologies possible to lessen the damage to the forest.

Some companies have responded to the environmentalists' demands. Today, a U.S. company named Occidental Petroleum is drilling for oil in Ecuador—a country whose rain forest suffered terribly under the old way of doing business. But Occidental is taking a different approach. The company is trying to create a model of how to extract oil from the rain forest in an environmentally sensitive way. At its production facilities, water and other by-products are carefully recycled. The company is funding local health clinics and schools and teaching farming techniques to villagers. According to one Occidental employee, the environmental movement "has changed the way we think. Back in the old days we did whatever we needed to do and just hid it." [41]

Unfortunately, many companies behave as if the "old days" are not over. Large Asian logging companies are flocking to the Amazon and threatening to pick up where the oil companies left off in the 1980s. The Malaysian timber firms currently negotiating to buy land in Brazil have gained a bad reputation for almost completely logging their own country. Eduardo Martins, president of IBAMA, awaits the arrival of the Malaysian companies worriedly: "What we fear is that they will do to the Amazon what they've already done to their own forests." [42]

Oil exploration in the Amazon will always come with an environmental cost, but Occidental's new approach is a step in the right direction. Just as the residents of the Amazon are being encouraged to use the land in a more sustainable way, large foreign corporations must be convinced that they should take better care of the Amazon's resources.

Lenders and borrowers

Because of their economic power, nations like the United States, Japan, France, Italy, and Germany have an enormous amount of influence over development in the

Some companies still practice destructive techniques such as slash-and-burn logging.

Amazon. If Bolivia wants to build a road into the Amazon, the chances are good that it will turn to a foreign bank for help. Without a bank loan, Bolivia probably would not have enough money to construct the road.

In many cases, the institution that Amazonian nations approach for a loan is the World Bank. The World Bank's mission is to promote economic growth and stability in growing nations. It has lent hundreds of millions of dollars to support the construction of dams, roads, and mines in the Amazon. In the past, however, these loans were made without taking the environmental effects of the projects into consideration.

For example, the World Bank's commitment of millions of dollars to Polonoroeste, a massive development program in Brazil, resulted in "the highest rate of deforestation in the world, threatening the ruin of a tropical forest area three-fourths the size of France."[43] The project also sparked a malaria epidemic and threatened the survival of forest tribes. Ultimately, the World Bank stopped supporting this project because of its high environmental cost.

The Sierra Club, Environmental Defense Fund, and other conservation organizations want the World Bank and other foreign banks to stop funding projects that destroy the Amazon. Responding to this pressure, the World Bank has made a number of changes in its lending practices. Loans are now reviewed by environmental experts before they are finalized, and an effort is made to support projects that are less harmful to the rain forest. The World Bank has also created a $400 million fund for projects that encourage sustainable use and forest protection.

Debt-for-nature

Big loans from foreign banks have also trapped Amazonian nations in a vicious cycle of debt. Their governments have borrowed vast sums of money for development projects. The countries owe millions of dollars, payment on loans they hoped would keep their economies growing. Because of inflation and other factors, it is unlikely that these nations will ever be able to repay these loans. Nor do they have money to create national parks and reserves or launch new conservation projects.

One of the most innovative solutions to this problem was developed by Thomas Lovejoy of the Smithsonian Institution. In a 1984 article in the *New York Times*, Lovejoy wrote: "The international debt crisis should remind us of the ecological as well as the economic links between rich and poor. Why not use the debt crisis . . . to help solve environmental problems."[44]

Lovejoy's article laid the groundwork for the debt-for-nature swap. The swap involves several steps. First, a portion of the country's commercial debt—money it owes to a bank—is purchased by a conservation group. The debt is normally bought at a discount because the bank feels that it has little chance of ever collecting the money.

The conservation group donates the debt to the central bank of the debtor country. The debtor country converts it into cash, which is then used to pursue conservation projects in the Amazon. Everyone involved comes out ahead. The bank is able to recover part of the money it is owed, and it receives a tax benefit for selling the debt at a discount. The debtor nation no longer owes as much money to the bank, and the conservation group ensures that part of the Amazon is protected.

Debt-for-nature is gaining popularity in the Amazon. In one of the first exchanges, Conservation International purchased $650,000 of Bolivian debt for $100,000. In return, the Bolivian government put money toward the expansion and maintenance of a rain forest reserve. In Ecuador the World Wildlife Fund purchased $10 million of that country's debt. The Ecuadorian government will in turn invest in park management and environmental education.

Lovejoy argues that debt-for-nature exchanges can work on an even larger scale. Foreign governments, with far more money to spend than conservation groups, could purchase giant amounts of debt and funnel the money to the conservation of the Amazon.

Debt-for-nature has its critics. Some argue that it takes advantage of poor nations, helping them to get rid of their debt but forcing them to spend money in ways that they do not control. Other environmentalists question whether the money is going to support conservation or, instead, to further development in the Amazon. The first swap with Bolivia was criticized both for continuing to allow the exploitation of the rain forest and for ignoring the needs of the native people living in the reserve.

While the debt-for-nature swap is not a perfect solution, it has been effective in promoting conservation. By giving Amazonian nations an economic incentive to preserve the rain forest, it takes aim at the root causes of deforestation.

Legal protections

As foreign nations take economic steps to support rain forest conservation, Amazonian nations must make changes to their laws and policies. For decades the Brazilian government has actively encouraged deforestation. Tax incentives for large corporations and landholders and weak environmental protection laws have added to the destruction.

Recently Brazil has made an effort to strengthen the legal protections for the rain forest. Early in 1998 the Brazilian Congress established regulations limiting forest burnings, logging, and large landholdings. At the same time, it announced that it would not issue any new licenses to log mahogany, and it canceled permits to loggers who were not using sustainable methods.

In the past, as environmental laws got tougher only the amount of legal logging decreased. Illegal logging increased, as did the overall amount of deforestation. Environmentalists worry that the new laws lack the enforcement and money needed to make them effective.

It is important to remember that a large percentage of the Brazilian population is not interested in conservation. Miners, loggers, and oil companies are well represented in the capitals of Amazonian nations, and they are putting pressure on the governments to open up more areas of the rain forest to development. These demands do not go unheeded. The Brazilian government is currently building a $1.2 billion surveillance satellite to pinpoint the location of minerals and other hidden treasures.

The future of the rain forest

Commenting on the future of the Amazon, ecologist Phillip Fearnside notes, "There's still time, it depends on what is done with it."[45] Indeed, fully 85 percent of the rain forest remains intact. In spite of the damage already done, the fight for the Amazon is far from over.

There is no single solution to the destruction of the Amazon. A massive effort on the part of governments, corporations, and individuals around the world will be required. Sacrifices both large and small will also have to be made: A poor Amazonian nation might have to resist the temptation to develop yet another piece of the rain forest; a timber company might be called upon to use logging techniques that are environmentally friendly instead of just cheap and fast; and a shopper in the United States or Europe might have to live without furniture made from Brazilian mahogany.

The rain forest cannot survive as long as it is exploited for commercial interests. Changes in the laws must be made and incentives created to discourage the abuse of the rain forest by large companies and landholders.

"...ON THE BRIGHT SIDE, THE ENDANGERED SPECIES LIST IS DOWN TO ONE."

For some, these sacrifices may seem large or even painful. It is not always easy to give something up when the future benefits of doing so are not immediately apparent. But whatever the price of saving the Amazon may be, it will be tiny in comparison to the ecological and scientific costs of allowing it to disappear. The fate of humans is closely tied to the fate of the forest and other natural areas like it.

There are ethical reasons to save the Amazon as well. The majestic and complex rain forest was in existence millions of years before humans began to roam the earth. As relative newcomers to the planet, we must be aware of our place within a much larger system. We are not only the beneficiaries of the earth's great wealth but the caretakers of it as well. If we destroy the Amazon and other natural areas for economic gain, we have failed in that role.

Notes

Chapter 1: Nature's Hothouse

1. Edward O. Wilson, "Rainforest Canopy: The High Frontier," *National Geographic*, December 1991, p. 92.

2. Quoted in Arnold Newman, *Tropical Rainforests: A World Survey of Our Most Valuable and Endangered Habitat with a Blueprint for Its Survival*. New York: Facts On File, 1990, p. 12.

3. Quoted in Barbara Bedway, "Life Above the Branches: Follow Your Nose to the Rainforest Canopy and Get a Bird's-Eye View of Earth's Most Diverse Ecosystem," *Science World*, January 12, 1996, p. 17.

4. Quoted in Lisa Silcock, ed., *The Rainforests: A Celebration*. San Francisco: Chronicle Books, 1992, p. 86.

5. Mark Collins, ed., *The Last Rain Forests: A World Conservation Atlas*. New York: Oxford University Press, 1990, p. 58.

6. Wilson, "Rainforest Canopy," p. 102.

Chapter 2: The Amazon in Peril

7. Quoted in Juan de Onis, *The Green Cathedral: Sustainable Development of Amazonia*. New York: Oxford University Press, 1992, p. 24.

8. Quoted in Susanna Hecht and Alexander Cockburn, *The Fate of the Forest: Developers, Destroyers, and Defenders of the Amazon*. London: Verso, 1989, p. 95.

9. Quoted in Dudley Althaus, "Black Gold, Broken Promise: Amazon's Empty Legacy, Ecuador's Toxic New World," *Houston Chronicle*, December 12, 1996, p. A1.

10. Martha C. Christian, ed., *Emerald Realm: Earth's Precious Rain Forests*. Washington, DC: National Geographic Society, 1990, p. 135.

11. Quoted in Neil Hollander and Robert MacLean, "Mud-Caked Amazon Miners Wallow in Newfound Wealth and Power," *Smithsonian*, April 1984, p. 88.

12. Quoted in Laurie Goering, "Rain Forest Residents Sue Texaco: Drilling Left Mess in Ecuadoran Jungle," *Washington Post*, July 16, 1996, p. A16.

13. Quoted in Goering, "Rain Forest Residents Sue Texaco," p. A16.

14. Quoted in Gabrielle Walker, "Kinder Cuts," *New Scientist*, September 21, 1996, p. 40.

15. Walker, "Kinder Cuts," p. 40.

16. Quoted in Marguerite Holloway, "Sustaining the Amazon," *Scientific American*, July 1993, p. 96.

17. Quoted in Anthony DePalma, "In Suriname's Rain Forests, a Fight over Trees vs. Jobs," *New York Times*, September 4, 1995, sec. 1, p. 1.

Chapter 3: The Price of Destruction

18. Quoted in Laurie Goering, "Blazes Char Amazon Forest," *Chicago Tribune*, October 17, 1997, news section, p. 1.

19. Quoted in Diana Jean Schemo, "Burning of Amazon Picks Up Pace, with Vast Areas Lost," *New York Times*, September 12, 1996, p. A3.

20. Quoted in Patrick Huyghe, "New Species Fever: To Preserve Biodiversity, Scientists Must Discover New Forms of Life Fast—Before They're Gone," *Audubon*, March/April 1993, p. 90.

21. Quoted in Jonathan Burton, "Paradise Lost? Threat of Destruction of South America's Amazon Rain Forest," *Scholastic Update*, vol. 125, no. 9, February 12, 1993, p. 21.

22. Quoted in Katie Rodgers, "Back to Our Roots: Searching for New Drugs in the Rain Forest," *Drug Topics*, vol. 139, no. 1, January 9, 1995, p. 58.

23. Quoted in Christian, *Emerald Realm*, p. 102.

24. Quoted in Andrea Dorfman, "Assault in the Amazon: Brazil Tries to Drive Gold Miners from the Rainforest Home

of the Stone Age Yanomami Tribe," *Time*, November 5, 1990, p. 100.

25. Quoted in Polly Ghazi, "The Continuing Fight for the Amazon," *World Press Review*, vol. 41, no. 9, September 1994, p. 46.

26. Quoted in Christian, *Emerald Realm*, p. 94.

27. Quoted in Roger D. Stone, *Dreams of Amazonia*. New York: Elisabeth Sifton Books-Viking, 1985, p. 154.

Chapter 4: The Fight for the Forest

28. Quoted in Diana Jean Schemo, "Rising Fires Renew Threat to Amazon," *New York Times*, November 2, 1997, p. A8.

29. Quoted in Christian, *Emerald Realm*, p. 121.

30. Quoted in Sy Montgomery, "Eden in the Amazon: Peru's 800,000-Acre Tamshiyacu-Tahuayo Reserve Brings Fresh Ideas to Rainforest Conservation," *Animals*, vol. 131, no. 1, January/February 1998, p. 14.

31. Quoted in Montgomery, "Eden in the Amazon," p. 15.

32. Quoted in Hecht and Cockburn, *The Fate of the Forest*, p. 227.

33. Quoted in Burton, "Paradise Lost?" p. 22.

34. Quoted in Stone, *Dreams of Amazonia*, p. 160.

35. Quoted in Christian, *Emerald Realm*, p. 166.

36. Quoted in Walker, "Kinder Cuts," p. 41.

37. Quoted in Stone, *Dreams of Amazonia*, p. 158.

38. Quoted in Gabrielle Walker, "Slash and Grow," *New Scientist*, September 21, 1996, p. 33.

Chapter 5: Global Solutions

39. Quoted in Jeremy Schlosberg, "Rain Forest Chic: Saving the Rain Forest Was the Hot Cause of the '80s, but Does Anyone Still Care?" *Vegetarian Times*, May 1995, p. 80.

40. Quoted in Schlosberg, "Rain Forest Chic," p. 80.

41. Quoted in Dudley Althaus, "Amazon's Empty Legacy—Big Oil Responds to the Environment," *Houston Chronicle*, December 15, 1996, p. A27.

42. Quoted in Tod Robberson, "Devastation Escalating in Brazil's Rain Forests—Alarmed Environmentalists Press for Solution," *Dallas Morning News*, December 22, 1997, p. 1A.

43. Suzanne Head and Robert Heinzman, eds., *Lessons of the Rainforest*. San Francisco: Sierra Club Books, 1990, p. 122.

44. Quoted in Christian, *Emerald Realm*, p. 184.

45. Quoted in Howard LaFranchi, "Spare the Ax, Spoil the Amazon," *Christian Science Monitor*, May 14, 1997, p. 9.

Glossary

agoutis: Large rodents that feed on nuts from the Brazil nut tree.

agroforestry: Farming in the rain forest that combines trees and crops, thus helping the forest to last.

biodiversity: The number of plant and animal species found within a given area.

bromeliads: A type of epiphyte capable of holding a gallon or more of water in a cup formed by its leaves.

canopy: The thick top layer of the rain forest, formed by interconnecting tree tops. Seventy-five percent of rain forest life lives in the canopy.

curare: A plant used by native hunters to stun their prey. It is also used by doctors performing complex surgery.

debt-for-nature swap: A new strategy for conserving the rain forest while reducing the debts of Amazonian nations.

decomposers: Insects that feed on dead plants and animals, digest the decaying matter, and release the stored nutrients.

deforestation: The loss of forest cover due to cutting or other causes.

dispersers: Monkeys, birds, and bats that spread fruit seeds throughout the forest.

ecotourist: A person who visits rain forests or other natural areas on vacation.

entomologist: A scientist who studies insect species.

epiphyte: Plants that cling to the trees in the canopy without relying on them for nutrients. Instead, they draw food and moisture from the bark of trees or directly from the air.

ethnobotany: The scientific study of how people who live in the rain forest use the plants around them.

evapotranspiration: The ecological process that returns rain caught by trees and plants to the atmosphere.

extractive reserve: An area that has been preserved for native people to harvest rain forest products such as rubber or Brazil nuts.

garimpeiro: An independent gold miner in the Brazilian Amazon.

greenhouse effect: The trapping of radiation in the atmosphere, resulting in increased temperatures. Gases such as carbon dioxide and methane speed this process.

liana: A large, woody vine that latches onto the trunks of tall trees to reach the sunlight.

manioc: A root vegetable found in the Amazon that now provides food to 300 million people around the world.

mycorrhiza: A threadlike combination of fungi and plant roots that covers tree roots, dead leaves, insects, and animals. Mycorrhiza breaks down and digests dead matter and returns stored nutrients to the trees.

photosynthesis: The conversion by green plants of the sun's energy into carbohydrates.

quinine: A drug used to treat malaria, first discovered in the bark of a rain forest tree.

seringuieros: Also known as rubber tappers; people who earn a living by collecting latex from the trunks of wild rubber trees.

shaman: A tribal doctor who uses plants to treat a variety of illnesses.

shifting cultivation: A sustainable method of farming that is used by many forest people.

sustainable use: The idea that humans can use a natural resource without destroying it.

World Bank: The bank that makes large loans to support construction projects in Brazil and other developing nations. The World Bank has been accused of funding projects without concern for the damage they cause to the Amazon.

Organizations
to Contact

Conservation International
1015 18th St., NW, Suite 1000
Washington, DC 20036
(202) 429-5660

Conservation International works to protect biodiversity and ecological systems worldwide.

Cultural Survival
11 Divinity Ave.
Cambridge, MA 02138
(617) 495-2562

Cultural Survival markets products harvested in the rain forest using sustainable methods.

Environmental Defense Fund
257 Park Ave. South
New York, NY 10010
(212) 505-2100

The Environmental Defense Fund addresses rain forest destruction, global warming, ocean pollution, and other global environmental issues.

National Wildlife Federation
1400 16th St. NW
Washington, DC 20036-2266
(202) 797-6800

The National Wildlife Federation promotes the conservation of natural resources and publishes *Ranger Rick* and *Big Backyard* magazines for children.

Natural Resources Defense Council
40 W. 20th St.
New York, NY 10011
(212) 727-2700

The Natural Resources Defense Council researches environmental problems and undertakes legal action on environmental issues.

Nature Conservancy
1815 N. Lynn St.
Arlington, VA 22209
(703) 841-5300

The Nature Conservancy protects biodiversity and endangered ecosystems worldwide.

Rainforest Action Network
450 Sansome St., Suite 700
San Francisco, CA 94111
(415) 398-4404
e-mail: rainforest@igc.apc.org

The Rainforest Action Network works to protect tropical forests in the United States and around the world.

Rainforest Alliance
65 Bleecker St.
New York, NY 10012
(212) 677-1900

The Rainforest Alliance produces educational materials and a newsletter about the rain forests and coordinates travel opportunities.

World Wildlife Fund
1250 24th St. NW
Washington, DC 20037
(202) 293-4800

The World Wildlife Fund protects the natural resources of Africa, Asia, and Latin America.

Suggestions for Further Reading

Joann J. Burch, *Chico Mendes: Defender of the Rain Forest*. Brookfield, CT: Millbrook Press, 1994. A biography of Chico Mendes, the man who helped lead the rubber tappers in their struggle for land rights in the Amazon.

Martha C. Christian, ed., *Emerald Realm: Earth's Precious Rain Forests*. Washington, DC: National Geographic Society, 1990. A collection of *National Geographic* articles about conservation, ecology, and human activities in rain forests around the world. Includes excellent photographs.

Susanna Hecht and Alexander Cockburn, *The Fate of the Forest: Developers, Destroyers and Defenders of the Amazon*. London: Verso, 1989. Thorough description of the causes of destruction in the Amazon, with an account of the ecological and cultural damage.

Daniel R. Katz and Miles Chapin, eds., *Tales from the Jungle: A Rain Forest Reader*. New York: Crown Trade Paperbacks, 1995. Essays about rain forests by explorers, adventurers, and scientists. Also includes short fiction written about rain forests.

Virginia Morell, "On the Origin of (Amazonian) Species," *Discover*, April 1997. Follows several naturalists as they attempt to uncover the causes behind the tremendous biodiversity in the Amazon.

Marion Morrison, *The Amazon Rain Forest and Its People*. New York: Thomson Learning, 1993. This book provides a description of the Amazon, the people who live within it, and the development activities taking place there.

Juan de Onis, *The Green Cathedral: Sustainable Development of Amazonia.* New York: Oxford University Press, 1992. Addresses the ways that governments, environmental organizations, and others are using the idea of sustainable use to conserve the Amazon.

Gabrielle Walker, "Slash and Grow," *New Scientist*, September 21, 1996. Traces researchers' efforts to develop better ways of farming in the Amazon. One of four articles about the Amazon in this issue.

Works Consulted

Dudley Althaus, "Amazon's Empty Legacy—Big Oil Responds to the Environment," *Houston Chronicle*, December 15, 1996.

———, "Black Gold, Broken Promise: Amazon's Empty Legacy, Ecuador's Toxic New World," *Houston Chronicle*, December 12, 1996.

Barbara Bedway, "Life Above the Branches: Follow Your Nose to the Rainforest Canopy and Get a Bird's-Eye View of Earth's Most Diverse Ecosystem," *Science World*, January 12, 1996.

James Brooke, "Rubber Trees Being Planted in Brazil, the Source," *New York Times*, July 9, 1995.

Jonathan Burton, "Paradise Lost? Threat of Destruction of South America's Amazon Rain Forest," *Scholastic Update*, vol. 125, no. 9, February 12, 1993.

Catherine Caulfield, *In the Rainforest*. New York: Alfred A. Knopf, 1985.

Mark Collins, ed., *The Last Rain Forests: A World Conservation Atlas*. New York: Oxford University Press, 1990.

Anthony DePalma, "In Suriname's Rain Forests, a Fight over Trees vs. Jobs," *New York Times*, September 4, 1995.

Andrea Dorfman, "Assault in the Amazon: Brazil Tries to Drive Gold Miners from the Rainforest Home of the Stone Age Yanomami Tribe," *Time*, November 5, 1990.

Polly Ghazi, "The Continuing Fight for the Amazon," *World Press Review*, vol. 41, no. 9, September 1994.

Laurie Goering, "Blazes Char Amazon Forest," *Chicago Tribune*, October 17, 1997.

———, "Rain Forest Residents Sue Texaco: Drilling Left Mess in Ecuadoran Jungle," *Washington Post*, July 16, 1996.

Michael Goulding, Nigel J. H. Smith, Dennis J. Mahar, *Floods of Fortune: Ecology and Economy Along the Amazon*. New York: Columbia University Press, 1996.

Judith Gradwohl and Russell Greenberg, *Saving the Tropical Forests*. Washington, DC: Island Press, 1988.

Francis Hallé, "A Raft atop the Rain Forest," *National Geographic*, October 1990.

Suzanne Head and Robert Heinzman, eds., *Lessons of the Rainforest*. San Francisco: Sierra Club Books, 1990.

Steven Hendrix, "Bolivia's Outpost of Hope," *International Wildlife*, vol. 27, no. 1, January/February 1997.

Paul Henley, *Yanomami—Masters of the Spirit World*. San Francisco: Chronicle Books, 1995.

Neil Hollander and Robert MacLean, "Mud-Caked Amazon Miners Wallow in Newfound Wealth and Power," *Smithsonian*, April 1984.

Marguerite Holloway, "Sustaining the Amazon," *Scientific American*, July 1993.

Patrick Huyghe, "New Species Fever: To Preserve Biodiversity, Scientists Must Discover New Forms of Life Fast—Before They're Gone," *Audubon*, March/April 1993.

Howard LaFranchi, "Spare the Ax, Spoil the Amazon," *Christian Science Monitor*, May 14, 1997.

Les Line, "New Branch of Primate Family Tree," *New York Times*, June 18, 1996.

Sy Montgomery, "Eden in the Amazon: Peru's 800,000-Acre Tamshiyacu-Tahuayo Reserve Brings Fresh Ideas to Rainforest Conservation," *Animals*, vol. 131, no. 1, January/February 1998.

Carol Kaesuk Moon, "Chocoholics Take Note: Beloved Bean in Peril," *New York Times*, May 4, 1998.

———, "Splendor in the Mud: Unraveling the Lives of Anacondas," *New York Times*, April 2, 1996.

Virginia Morell, "Looking for Big Pink: South America's River Dolphins Are Disappearing, but Vera da Silva Is Out to Change That," *International Wildlife*, vol. 27, no. 6, November/December 1997.

Peggy Morgan, "The Pasha of Plants," *Prevention*, vol. 49, no. 1, January 1997.

Arnold Newman, *Tropical Rainforests: A World Survey of Our Most Valuable and Endangered Habitat with a Blueprint for Its Survival*. New York: Facts On File, 1990.

Tod Robberson, "Devastation Escalating in Brazil's Rain Forests—Alarmed Environmentalists Press for Solution," *Dallas Morning News*, December 22, 1997.

Katie Rodgers, "Back to Our Roots: Searching for New Drugs in the Rain Forest," *Drug Topics*, vol. 139, no. 1, January 9, 1995.

Diana Jean Schemo, "Burning of Amazon Picks Up Pace, with Vast Areas Lost," *New York Times*, September 12, 1996.

———, "Rising Fires Renew Threat to Amazon," *New York Times*, November 2, 1997.

Jeremy Schlosberg, "Rain Forest Chic: Saving the Rain Forest Was the Hot Cause of the '80s, but Does Anyone Still Care?" *Vegetarian Times*, May 1995.

Lisa Silcock, ed., *The Rainforests: A Celebration*. San Francisco: Chronicle Books, 1992.

Roger D. Stone, *Dreams of Amazonia*. New York: Elisabeth Sifton Books-Viking, 1985.

Laura Tangley, *The Rainforest*. New York: Chelsea House, 1992.

Gabrielle Walker, "Kinder Cuts," *New Scientist*, September 21, 1996.

Edward O. Wilson, "Rainforest Canopy: The High Frontier," *National Geographic*, December 1991.

Index

Picture Credits

About the Author

Darv Johnson is a writer living and working in Brooklyn, New York. Growing up in Chapel Hill, North Carolina, he developed an avid interest in wildlife and took many trips with his family to national parks throughout the United States. He attended the University of North Carolina, where he wrote his senior thesis about the forests of the Pacific Northwest. His growing interest in the conservation of natural resources led him to Washington, D.C., where he worked for a nonprofit conservation organization. There, he raised money to support fish and wildlife conservation in the United States, Canada, and Latin America. Most recently, he worked for a salmon conservation organization in Seattle, Washington.